How NOT to RV

A Few of the Many Glowing Reviews for <u>How NOT to RV</u>:

I am so loving your book ... I am laughing so hard my eyes are leaking. It is wonderful! Thank you indeed for a happy start to my day. - *Catherine R.*

I can't remember the last time I grabbed a book for "a little casual reading" and found myself on the last page, at 6AM, WISHING THERE WAS MORE!!!

For anyone who has had already had their first few forays out in the new/old RV (you definitely need a few miles under your belt to fully understand the sarcasm), this book is for you! Read it cover to cover while taking notes, have your wife or significant other do the same, review your notes, bring this book as a desk reference on your next journey through life in an RV and avoid the mistakes the rest of us make! This is definitely a "How To", just presented in reverse and in a far funnier fashion than I would have.

It is amazing how many similar circumstances Jennifer, a single woman from New York and myself, a married guy (20 years) living in Flagstaff, AZ, find ourselves in on the road. Yeah, we may have messed up in different places, sometimes even in different ways, but I can't even imagine how many embarrassing incidents I would have avoided had I read this (and had she gotten on the road sooner!) "way back when".

I can't say enough, incredible job Doc and HEY YOU, Buy This Book! – *Frank P.*

I love your book!! ... thanks again for encouraging us (solo women campers) to know we can and SHOULD if we dream of it. ... I love it so much …. thank you again! – *Linda G.*

Well, Well, Well and Boy Howdy! Just finished reading your book, … absolutely wonderful writing and a joy to read…many resonating points with us and our adventures with Betsy, our RV … thank you for writing your wonderful book – *Alex D.*

Greatly enjoyed reading your exploits. I am just about to embark on my second leg of my whirlwind tour of the great U S of A. ... I'd really love to get an audio version of this book. See ya down the road. - *Leonard S.*

I read your book in preparation for my trip, and am tickled pink that there's a place for us to share stories! – *Pat M.*

I just finished "How Not To RV" and was fascinated from beginning to end. I was searching for books on RVing on Amazon when I came across yours ... Thanks for the laughs and for validating our decision to embrace the RV experience, if only by baby steps for now. - *Brian M.*

Jennifer starts with a life changing decision, a moment of enlightenment, that opens her up to an adventure of a life time. With hilarious mishaps and thought provoking reflections she concludes the launch phase with, "let the evening air cascade onto your bare skin. Listen to the murmuring of the other campers around their campfire and the dog sniffling in the garbage. Sleep well my little hero, you have done a great thing." Indeed! ... Eventually, this trip, and what a trip it is, takes her to the doorstep of the adventure she had been looking for all along - but that will be in the next book. – *Pascal S.*

Fun on the Road with Dr. Jennifer – a real hoot! I had a great time reading (and laughing out loud) about how NOT to RV. I'm already an RVer and the book actually made me feel like winging it a little more on the road than we do, we're always so careful. It was lots of fun reading of Dr. Flower's exploits on a road certainly much less traveled out of New York City! It made me wonder if there might be a sequel. – *Roger C.*

Funniest bumpy ride ever. How NOT to RV, chapter after chapter, is the most entertaining "guide" a road warrior could hope for. And if you're not a road warrior, you'll either want to be or thank yourself for your good judgment after reading Jennifer Flower's hilariously astute account of her journey. Stand-up comics, take note. I hope she goes on another trip soon -- I want more of her stories. - *Suzanna S.*

How NOT to RV

An RVer's Guide to RVing in the Absurd

& Bonus Book:

How NOT to RV Redux:

For the RVer Who Never Learns

Jennifer Flower, Ph.D

These are How-NOT-to Guides, for readers conquering fear one failure at a time

These books are not intended as a substitute for good advice. Taking them literally will get you into a heap of trouble. If you are seriously considering following the instructions in these guides, you should see a psychologist, but probably not Dr. Jennifer Flower.

ISBN-13: 9780983995371
ISBN-10: 0983995370
Library of Congress Control Number: 2016921607
Bumpity Bump Publishing, Sausalito, CA

To my motyho

who took me where I needed to go

and to my sweetheart, Joe Flower

who is apparently where I was going.

Table of Contents

BOOK 2 How NOT to RV Redux: RVing for the RVer Who Never Learns

Introduction

I have spent some of the best times of my life in the motyho. That's what I call her. She's a 1986 Airstream motor home, a 345. That's thirty-four-and-a-half-feet of vintage Need This, Fix That. I'd drive, fix something, stop for gas, drive, fix something, stop for gas. Notice a pattern? It may not sound great to you, but it was heaven to me. But of course, that's not the whole story.

I didn't have a great time without getting myself into a few pickles on the road. If you're planning an RV adventure you should probably learn to like pickles no matter what kind of rig you're driving. Every RVer runs into The Unexpected and, in fact, many RVers go RVing for just that purpose.

The thing is, the surprises don't come how and when you'd predict.

Be careful what you wish for. Then make sure to appreciate the adventure part when it happens.

Now, don't get me wrong. I will go to my death defending my Airstream. Those vehicles are a marvel of engineering and design, sleek, like an airplane fuselage, the color of silver. In my rig's day, she was what travel looked like to people who wanted to do it in style. No Airstream needs an apologist. This rig was just a little over the hill, an old dream machine and a fitting vehicle for a woman having a midlife crisis.

When I started out I knew that my very big and very old motor home was sure to break down, possibly in expensive ways. For me, that was part of the adventure. I was in no hurry, I had no agenda, and I had fallen in love with an Airstream and wanted to invest in her. I knew that the breakdowns would involve me with people I would never have met otherwise. I may be nuts, but that sounded like fun to me.

So that was the point. After all the years of being so damn predictable in my life as a psychoanalyst, I set out to be totally unpredictable ... and accomplished exactly that.

It was a big risk to leave the people I loved and the professional life I'd built for an uncertain path and an unknown destination. But it was worth it. The trip I took and where it took me have brought me more joy than I would ever have predicted. It helped me find a life with a loving man, sharing his warm and talented family, and living in new and beautiful places.

So, if you're stuck in your life, here's the prescription: First you smell the coffee, *then* you smell the flowers.

You're going to be the beneficiary of my mistakes. I have excellent qualifications to write the How-NOT-To Guide you have here. I can instruct you, step by step, in how to create a journey full of problems, breakdowns, bad ideas, and generally stupid mistakes ... and still have an experience that can change your life. That you'll cherish. No, really.

This is truly an instruction manual. It's not full of little sugary stories about how charming and perfect things are. It's really how NOT to do it and I can get extremely specific on the subject. So prepare to learn and read between the lines.

Remember: We all make mistakes. We all forget stuff, have bad luck, and trip on something every now and then. I've spent most of my adult life helping people who can't live fully because they are afraid to screw up and look like an idiot. The same fear has kept me back more than I can say. The challenge – and you KNOW it – is to get out there and live anyway because sooner or later there will be no more stories to tell, no more dreams to be dreamt, and no more breaths to take.

So never mind what your friends are going to say or whether you'll screw up because – and here's the best part – the mistakes will happen all by themselves, *wherever you are*. You don't even have to work at those. Isn't that a relief? You don't have to make sure the mistakes will happen. Cross that off your list of things to do.

You may think you're not much of a risk taker. But look at it this way: Playing it safe is extremely risky! It's like putting your money under the mattress instead of investing it in something that will grow. The costs of living (in every sense of the phrase) reduce the value of your money and your life force. If you don't invest in the future, if you don't invest in yourself, that is the riskiest of all. You just end up having and being less and less.

The key thing to remember is, if you invest in yourself, You Will Grow.

And when or if you go back to the life you left, you'll have more of you to make the rest of your life with.

There is no moral to this story. Morals take the fun out of things. Doing exactly what I did is not even a good idea, as you'll see. But if you're stuck or you keep wishing for something, there's a good idea out there. Look for it. And you'll find a lot of other people out there who are doing it too, with all the screw-ups and the laughs that come with them.

Best of all, when you have a travel tale or two of your own to tell we've got a way for you to share it. On our website we have a very special place where you can tell us how you screwed up thoroughly, royally, and yes, proudly, on your personal mission to laugh in the face of destiny. At HowNOTtoRV.com/tellit we'd love to hear your wacky tale of woe. And if we get enough good ones (that we may edit for the utmost in writerly wackiness) we will publish these in a companion volume and you will get a free copy and a hat that asserts that you are, indeed, officially, "A How-NOT-to Guide."

For the more ambitious among you, it's also possible to become an Elite How-NOT-to Guide by writing one of our How-NOT-to Guides on another topic. Find out more at HowNOTtoRV.com/elite. You may have a future in the Self-Hindrance literature!

Remember: my story is Travel in the Absurd. It's a worst-case scenario written for people who insist on expecting the worst so they won't be disappointed. If anything close to this happens to you, that would be pretty darned impressive. So go ahead and dream of how much fun *your* trip will be when instead of disasters you get easy peasy all the way.

So, listen up! In case you are contemplating a radical change or even if you're just one of those people who enjoy other people's goofs, here are relatively clear instructions on how *not* to do what I did but how to Boldly Go anyway; how to upset one apple-cart and take another on the road.

PART ONE

Convincing Others... And Yourself

1

Why RV? Why Not Just Stay in a Hotel?

I was asked by my New York City friends many times, "Why go in an RV? Why don't you just camp in a tent?" (meaning, buy overpriced camping clothes and high-tech equipment), "Or stay in hotels?" (meaning, go only to charming B&Bs in artsy hamlets), "I know a lot of people around the U.S. You could stay with them" (meaning, why bother with all the fuss? You could be around people we know ... and you don't know what you're doing anyway!)

Those are fair questions. I'm not really sure I know the answers to why NOT those other things. All I know is:

You really need an RV when you want to sleep in parking lots, overhear other people's TVs, and compete for basic services like room in the communal garbage can.

You really need an RV if you like to play the slot machines – in the gas station. Every time you pull in to fuel up, it's anyone's guess what the price will be for, say, 80 gallons of gas. Think about that.

You really need an RV if what you *want* to do is spend an hour on either side of a day-on-the-road making and breaking camp. A motor home is a big house in motion and a lot like the home you left; if you don't pay attention, it will leak ugly juices. Unlike your home without wheels, if you don't pay attention, your RV will drag parts of the campground with you.

But you also need an RV if you live to drive, if you love getting to know a vehicle and all its quirks, if you crave the feeling of being at home wherever you are but can turn on a dime (if it's a pretty big dime) for a wooded glade or the nearest Airstream convention.

You need an RV if you want to be a host, if you want to offer the people you love an experience they would never have otherwise and with a lot of creature comfort.

And you need an RV if you want to wake up to new faces and accents and ready conversation seated in the security of each others' back yards.

You just need an RV for some things. Not everyone likes to sleep on the ground.

2

How to Flummox Your Friends and Colleagues

Tell them you're really going to do this trip thing; you're going to drop everything, just for a while. Tell them that you're going to leave your family, your job, your role as Ole Reliable, all for a 6-month trip. Tell yourself it will be a 6-month trip. Watch as their foreheads wrinkle, their eyeballs bulge, and the phrase forms on their lips, "Buh-, buh-, but…."

Notice that to some city dwellers, leaving in an RV on a long trip is about equivalent to joining the circus. But remember that paying half your income for a tiny apartment, standing in line in grey, littered streets for your morning coffee, and working a 70-hour week is not entirely rational to some. Admit that the circus is where we all live, one way or another, and joining it could just be your way of waking up.

And oh yes, the ultimate how NOT to? Sell your home or your office that you've just spent a lot of time and money renovating. Never mind if it's a bad market for selling.

Keep telling yourself it's just a 6-month trip.

PART TWO

The Mechanics of the Thing

3

How NOT to Buy an RV

Let's see, there are so many options to choose from.

You can get a little 16-foot Airstream Bambi trailer, streamlined aluminum inside and out with the retro look of the classic Airstreams in the '50s. You can get an Empress motor coach with living space that compares well with many homes around the country. You can get an old converted Greyhound with imperfectly fitted cabinetry that squeaks when you turn, and you can get a million-dollar rig with In-Motion Satellite Internet and a bath tub for two.

Most people start with the larger expense, a motor home or the trailer they want to pull with their gigantic pick-up. What I did of course was exactly the opposite. Here, I can say, after much practice and experimentation, is how NOT to do it:

First, fall in love with a car without making sure that your particular motor home can tow it easily. I was forced to buy the Mini Cooper S in bright electric blue when she followed me out of the showroom, starred in my dreams of adventure, and hovered mid-air in my office accompanied by a choir of angels while patients nearby told me their sorry tales. If you *have* to buy the car first, then ...

Sure, laboriously research every coach on the market. Entertain wild ideas that you can't afford like a motor home with a garage in the back for your Toad (that's what they call the vehicle you're towing – don't you love that?) Yes, there are companies that make motor homes big enough to carry your car in the cargo hold. Then call the manufacturers, go to the RV shows ... and ignore most of what you learn ...

Because one day it happens.

Go to a bleak, grey RV sales lot in central New Jersey. Fall in love with an old coach the likes of which you've never seen before. Notice her long, curvaceous lines … very, very long, much longer than anything you've ever driven before and much longer than you need. Notice the shine of her aluminum skin, the alluring, if glazed look in her headlights. Hear an out-of-tune Mariachi band playing while you are standing on the asphalt gazing at the vehicle. Demand to see her even though someone just brought her in for resale only an hour ago.

Stroke the dated upholstery, the dirty kitchen counter. Sit in the driver's seat, turn the key in the ignition and listen to the throaty, carbureted engine and burst into laughter. As your blood pressure rises and your face flushes, cast about for an off-hand remark to make to the salesman, like "You gotta sell this to me or it's curtains for you!" Only then ask how much she is and what's wrong with her. Fortunately, you know it couldn't be anywhere near as much as the wacky rigs you've been considering so, by comparison, you're getting a bargain. Right? Hmmmm.

Really look at the motor home. Notice only the finishes and the fact that she is extremely cool. Fantasize about how you will drive into town and your friends will gape in amazement, think of the hip retro parties you will give in her, the fun you will have furnishing and renovating her, the sexy encounters you will have in the bedroom once you have converted the twins into a huge bed the width of the vehicle. Then pay the full asking price and take her off the lot before they've even had a chance to fully inspect her. Yes, really, that's how (NOT) to do it.

4

How NOT to Drive Your Motor Home the First Time. Or Ever, Really.

Jump in the driver's seat, snap on your pointless seatbelt and steer your new rig toward your hometown dealer for repairs, making sure once you get on the road to whoop and holler at the highest possible volume. Forget which bridge or tunnel crossing will accommodate a 34.5-foot coach over ten feet tall. Realize you have no idea how your motor home is classified and whether she will fit where you're driving her. Break out into a sweat. Make sure to whoop and holler some more anyway. Head for the George Washington Bridge crossing all your fingers and toes.

As you drive up to the tollbooth, regard the No Hazardous Materials sign with horror. Yes, you do have a propane tank onboard. And no, you have no clue as to whether there is any propane in it or whether it matters. Prepare yourself to be arrested either for reckless endangerment or terrorism. Wipe away the sweat streaming into your eyes as the toll-taker regards you with disinterest.

Laugh giddily as you drive over a beautiful bridge with a stunning view of one of the most exciting cities in the world. Marvel that you are so high up you see over the railing. But keep your eyes on the road because you aren't really that sure which highways you're allowed to travel. And since there's nothing like your vehicle on the road for about a 500-mile radius, you have absolutely no basis for judging by comparison.

Wave and flash all the drivers who are waving and flashing you.

When the door to the bathroom swings open completely blocking your view through the back window, ignore the fact that you have a back-up camera (that tells you what's behind you) and struggle to see everything using your side mirrors. Reflect philosophically on the fact that they are positioned incorrectly and you now have little information for lane changes. Notice that your left (signaling) arm is very short relative to the size and length of the vehicle.

Feeling the road is yours even though you can't see most of it, open the window expansively and watch the side curtain blow straight out. Notice the loud flapping sound and wonder whether you can continue the two-hour drive listening to it. Try to pull it back in while you are driving and attempt to fasten all the snaps with one hand. Sing to yourself, "Driver's Ed! Driver's Ed!" remembering all the movies in Driver's Education of very stupid drivers dying spectacularly while attempting maneuvers like this.

Try to catch the items that are now falling all over the coach.

Turn on the radio. Notice that most of the sounds are unintelligible. Think of all the money you will pour injudiciously into the sound system. Salivate.

Now, mind you, this is just the first hour of owning a motor home.

5

How NOT to Service Your RV

Time passes quickly, what with all the distractions, and your drive is ending as you pull into your local Airstream dealer who will advise you about what your aging coach needs. The service manager's eyes shine as he sees you coming. You think it's just the cold wind in his face.

Here's how NOT to save money preparing your motor home for the road:

Develop a punch list (as in, Punch Driver in Wallet).

Let's see, there's the all-points inspection, the fans in the bathroom, you could install a Banks exhaust system for extra power to tow your Toad, service the generator (what's the generator for?), install an auxiliary braking system in the Toad and a high quality hitch, add a new audio source unit with remote control and a few new speakers to the sound system.

What's left? Oh, there's replacing the entire carpet with trendy wool wall-to-wall. Yes, I actually did say put wool wall-to-wall carpet in your motor home. A very bad idea.

Of course there's the swiveling spotlight on top, gotta have that.

And that comes to what, $11,000? Who said that? Did I say that's a third of the value of the entire, aging vehicle? Hey! At least I saved a lot when I bought a used one.

6

A Walking Tour of the Motyho

Yes, that's what I call her, the motyho. Don't ask me how I arrived at that.

In this chapter I will not instruct but will simply show why I, in particular, was compelled to attempt this folly of circumnavigating the country in a vintage vehicle that, though once an icon of modern design and fine engineering, was clearly a little worse for wear.

For a do-it-yourselfer, of course, such a project would have been merely a labor of love. For me it was a labor of love, but it was going to have to be my love and someone else's labor.

You might have trouble understanding why someone who had never changed the oil in anything would undertake a trip like this in a vintage vehicle. Others will immediately grasp the urgency to do it. She's an Airstream after all, and despite her age, she is hot!

I couldn't shake the picture of this gleaming chariot towing a Mini. I knew that no matter where I drove my aging rig, no matter how stuck I got, my Mini would take me to safety. The Mini's got plenty of power, she's a beautifully crafted machine, and has more personality than some people I know. But not more personality than my Silver Bullet. So did I throw caution to the winds for the sake of appearance (well, and fine engineering)? You bet I did. It's hard to get the New York out of the New Yorker and believe me, many have tried.

Let's take a walk through the motyho as she was before she'd embarked on an epic journey with me.

Approach the vehicle from the curbside because this is the only place you'll find a door. No hopping out of a street-side driver's door in emergencies for this cowgirl.

You're climbing a set of metal steps that retract and extend automatically when the engine is running but which can be fixed in either position once you figure out which of the three million toggle switches operate it. One switch is for the light over the door, another is for the light on the side of the motor home – I believe it's for the purpose of blinding oncoming visitors – and the rest, well, it was too hard to keep track.

The door looks like something you'd see on the side of an airplane; it's curved, with a little rounded window in it and a pull-shade that is neatly seated between the exterior and interior walls. You've never owned a door that curved on purpose.

Open the door. Yeah, it squeaks a little. There's the doormat with the Airstream name and the hip wool carpet that came at a very, very high price (more about this later). Immediately to your left is a tambour wood magazine rack for emergency-reading needs on your way in and out of the coach. There's also the carbon monoxide sensor that you'd better make damn sure works real good.

Straight ahead is the foldout sofa upholstered in a dated floral pattern that must have been unique to this line. It's a velveteen medley of buffs and mauves that is deceptively tough but still hosts a few cigarette burns. Nice touch. Imagine, correctly, that you will spend many hours lying on this very comfy couch, reading and thinking, zephyrs stirring the missed hairs on the leg you've slung up onto the window sill.

If you turn right and look two steps up you will see the driver's and passenger's flesh-colored leather swivel chairs. These are the chairs you worked over with Comet at the urging of the detail lady at the dealer. Yes, I said Comet. On leather. The chairs are clearly indestructible.

You can turn these chairs almost all the way around to pretend you would be comfortable conversing with people sitting two steps down in the living room. (But by the time you are in these chairs, all you want to do is DRIVE.) There's the doghouse between them. That's the hump that hides the motor, thoughtfully located inside the cabin thereby exposing you to the rumbles and odors of a ripe old engine but allowing for much more room inside.

On the curbside, opposite the sofa, you'll see two dirty pink barrel chairs fore and aft of a small table with copper metallic laminate on top. You can pull a large tabletop up from the back of this table that makes for tight seating but better eating. Very efficient, a great use of space.

So far so good.

Turn around. Astern of the foldout sofa is the dinette, upholstered in the same period fabric. The dinette tabletop folds down into a bed for those of us who are very short or like sleeping with our knees up our noses. Behind the dinette on the wall facing forward is a mirror. If you turn around fast from the driver's seat in a moment of disorientation, you will see yourself looking very confused.

On the curbside opposite the dinette is the kitchenette. There's a stainless steel sink amply stained, a four-burner propane stovetop laced with grease, and set into the worn Formica countertop the crowning but inoperable flush-mounted blender motor! Very 60s. Good for accumulating soggy crumbs.

Directly behind the kitchenette is the shower and across from the shower are the toilet and sink. The Corian counter is tastefully curved around the compact sink and the toilet is a little complicated. (More about that later.)

Behind each of these units on either side are closets with almost plenty of room for your belongings, and behind these is a set of twin beds, soon to be Rube Goldberged into a wall-to-wall bed allowing free rolling when the vehicle is in motion. Not wise but fun. There is a ribbon of windows curving all the way around the back, a shelf along the back wall, and, in the overhead cabinets, audio speakers so old they merely whisper.

The w/c is enclosed with a wooden door that, when swung into the hallway, can be locked in place to create a private master bedroom/bathroom. The door has a little, tiny peephole.

Light-stained oak cabinets stretch the length of the coach overhead and underneath. There are many, many windows.

To me, it's totally cool.

Now, what my friends do when they come to visit is they flop down on the furniture, ask where we are going, and request tropical drinks.

7

How NOT to Equip Yourself
for a Mere Road Trip

It's really worth doing some research. Here's how to overdo it:

Read books, visit RV websites, join forums on RV travel, talk with technicians about satellite equipment, and interview friends about great places to visit.

Then get serious: chart 3 million possible routes, try to predict weather patterns months in advance, review tirelessly and repeatedly until your family begs you for mercy the sole two videos on how to operate a motor home …

Let's see, what did I leave out?

Oh. Procure tools you don't know how to use, buy repair guides you don't understand, and sign up for two, count 'em, two emergency road service contracts.

All classic newbie behavior and the object of ridicule by any true explorer.

8

The Big (Sort-Of) Day or, How NOT To Have a Going Away Party

The time for the launch has arrived. Friends are coming from hundreds of miles. One couple brings their little Shasta trailer and camps out nearby on the lawn. There is great frivolity. Even the Canada geese restrain their output for the occasion. For some reason everything is terribly funny. People are excited about what you're doing and enjoy the chance to participate in the Big Breakout. There's a lot of fantasizing about other adventures we can take, ways we can change our lives.

In the morning, prepare to get underway. Turn the key in the ignition. Turn the key in the ignition again. Speculate on the likelihood that friends have sabotaged your departure. Thank them ambivalently in your mind.

Resign yourself to another two weeks of work on the coach. Wave goodbye to the guests instead of having the guests wave goodbye to you.

9

How NOT to Reassure Your Friends

Most of my friends were a little skeptical about my trip. It's not fair to blame them. New Yorkers tend to travel in the mind or in Europe; they don't have much truck with sewer hose.

Mostly, they were concerned about me; I've always been a bit of an oddball but this proposal of mine to throw everything up in the air was pretty radical. I had told them I'd be back soon but they had pointed out, "But Jenni! You SOLD your apartment!"

Was I burning my bridges? Would I be safe?

On one of those days when we were still trying to solve the straggling problems, my friend Paul, a psychoanalyst like me, very attentively and handily helped me with many of the small details. I could see that he was getting increasingly concerned, the more repairs we found the motor home still needed and the more inadequate our solutions were becoming.

As the time to go neared I discovered that I couldn't budge one of the storage bays. Paul suggested that maybe I should delay my trip, what with all the problems remaining to be solved.

I insisted they were minor and that the time was now or never.

Paul, who was already down on all fours trying to unstick the drawer himself, realized he couldn't do it either, and finally threw his arms around my knees and begged,

"Are you sure you have to do this? Jenni, please don't go!"

How can you leave a friend like that? You invite him on your trip when the time is right.

10

How NOT to Leave First Thing in the Morning the Way You're Supposed To

Go ahead. Just try to tie up all the loose ends before leaving. First the small things, then the larger things, then the small things, then the larger things ... The summer is getting hotter, and the trip is starting to feel like an anticlimax. Realize that you have achieved what you set out to, that you've bought an unpredictable machine and that it's going to be unpredictable, even when you don't feel like it. Congratulate yourself on your courage and inventiveness.

Finally, the day arrives again. You've made all the repairs you're going to make. You check the oil, the tire pressure, make sure the storage bays are locked. Fasten the awnings at the top and bottom, shut the rear windows, close the ceiling fan lids, stow everything that moves, the toaster, the tea kettle, the dishwashing soap, the cooking utensils, the water jug, the plants, the telephone, the printer, the stack of books, the maps, all the slippery objects that will slip no matter where you put them. Put the spillables on the shower floor.

If you're a psychoanalyst, take little plastic Freud off his pedestal (well, actually, you did that long ago). Put him in the side window so he can wave to passing cars. Seat the beanie baby (a going-away gift) on the rear-view mirror to remind you that behind you are people who love you.

Then spend ten minutes hitching the Mini because you have to keep getting out of the car to see how close you've gotten to the motor home. Make sure not to have a friend or neighbor on hand to help you because they would have saved a lot of time. Get grease all over you because you've forgotten to keep your gloves on. Forget how to connect the auxiliary braking system. Do it right anyway: connect the wires under the Toad hood for the turn signals, hook the auxiliary brake pedal onto the car's brake pedal, drain the air bladder, calibrate the breaking sensitivity, plug the run-away-alert monitor into the cigarette lighter.

Picture what you would do if, in fact, the Mini did loosen herself from the rig and return to New York due to homesickness.

Back in the coach, adjust the rear view mirrors the way they taught you, so that an object moves uninterruptedly from the rear-view to the flat, curbside mirror to the convex side-mirror, to the back-up camera to the driver's side-mirror. Oh, stop grousing about having to get up from the driver's seat every time you need to make an adjustment.

For the seventeenth time, climb back in the motor home and close the door, listening for the stairs to retract automatically. Bolt the door and get into the driver's seat. Put on your pointless seat belt. Look through the side mirror; look through the other side mirror. Then look at the backup camera and see your pert, snub-nosed Mini nuzzling the coach and waiting patiently to be led. Start the engine. Burst out laughing. Turn on the radio; Nothing In Particular comes on and it's music to your ears.

Let the engine warm up while you zone out for a minute. The lake is rippling peacefully, the geese are waiting for their next opportunity to poop on the lawn. Put her in gear and give the Mini a little tug to make sure the hitch engages properly. She clicks. Then give her some gas and feel the rig straighten and tense. Look at the Mini in the rear-view mirror and say, "OK Mini, let's go!" Give her a lot more gas, listen to the engine strain and set the whole 50-foot assembly into motion.

Burst into tears.

Drive about 40 feet. Then realize there really is no way you're going to get 50 feet of machinery through the narrow gate from this angle. This means you have to get out of the rig and disconnect the car because you can't back up while towing without damaging the coach transmission. Attempt to disconnect the Mini without tools, split open your thumb, and then assemble every possible tool you could need. Accumulate much more grease all over yourself. Wave wordlessly to joggers who pass by with astonished and inquiring looks.

When the rig is uncoupled, spend about ten minutes tearing up sod and twisting holes in the melting asphalt as you squeak the coach onto the two-lane road. Wonder whether the scars in the blacktop will still be there when you return and whether the town will fine the family.

Wonder when you will return.

After much maneuvering you get the coach onto the road. This is truly a good omen. Spend 10 more minutes rehitching the Mini.

Try to remember whether the coach water pump should be on or off. Realize that you hadn't closed the main propane valve! Thank God you had to stop to get the whole rig out of the drive-way ... or else you might have had a little 'splosion!

OK. Finally, it's time for the real thing. You have a rough idea where you're going tonight but by this point in the day you no longer have as much time to get there. Decide that this is not a problem and pull out into traffic. Notice that there isn't any traffic, you just like the sound of the phrase.

Roll past neighbors and familiar views, down the rural road, and through the little town in Connecticut. Then give her some serious gas.

* * * * * What a f * * * ing blast! * * * * *

Everything looks different from up here, it's like riding on top of a float at the Thanksgiving Day parade. The Airstream drives like a couch on a magic carpet; it's comfortable but unexpectedly responsive and aerodynamic even fully loaded. You can't believe they ever stopped making this one. The Mini is obediently, devotedly following close behind like a blue baby elephant, the radio crackles and a good signal finally comes in, the silverware drawer that doesn't lock is rolling open and closed with the turns and its contents jingle pleasantly.

We're making for western Pennsylvania, the day is clear and warm and the engine hums with little strain. Gradually the ride firms as the air suspension recharges. This is your new home.

You're a turtle with a spectacular shell towing a hare.

11

You're Motorin' Now or, How NOT to Take Yourself Too Seriously

When our forefathers crossed this great nation many years ago, they beat back the forests and braved foul weather and uncertainty of all kinds. They trusted each other as far as they could and did a lot with a little.

What they undertook bears no relationship to what you are doing. Here you are pulling many thousands of dollars of relatively high-end – if seasoned – equipment, and are carrying far more than you need for a few people, let alone one person.

You have maps on your devices, computer chips in your circuitry, and both the AAA and Good Sam's Emergency Road service watching your back. Despite a few errors in judgment, you are absurdly well prepared. You have researched your equipment and your possible routes on the Internet, you have read many books and viewed several videos on how to buy, operate, and maintain your rig. You are in instant communication by cell phone.

But can you be forgiven that occasional flash of excitement, the delight in discovery that every explorer must feel underway? Can you take any pride and satisfaction at all that at least something will surprise you and many things will be learned?

You bet your ass you can.

12

How NOT to Plan for the First Campground

Halfway across the state, a light rain begins, but no problem. It's just that the windshield wipers are old and somewhat less than enthusiastic. They move at independent speeds and the one on the right is starting to stick. Of course, you run out of fluid in the wiper wells so the road takes on a back-and-forth sort of quality. The radio reception blurs a little, too. It's time for an audiobook.

Did you know that audiobooks improve visibility?

By the time you decide to camp, the drive has gone so well you have forgotten that any unusual effort is required with respect to your rig. You are reminded, as you pull over to make a phone call, that you can't drop in at just any campground; many state parks have a length limit and there's no guarantee you'd be able to get in and out easily anyway.

In fact, you realize that you have to know which questions to ask the campground manager when you call ahead for a space, but you're not really sure what the questions are. Maybe it's, "How wide is the front gate?" Or possibly, "Are there any low-hanging tree-boughs?"

In order to finesse the problem, you choose a campground from the campground directory that welcomes big rigs. They must have room for you and it won't be quite so painfully obvious, mostly to you, that you still don't really know what you're doing.

Yay. They have a pull-through site in an RV park near the Delaware River. You know how to pull through. You won't even have to unhook the Mini, you'll be able to drive right out in the morning.

When you get there, the place looks clean and orderly, nothing fancy, the other campers are mostly tucked in for the night but a few are still sitting by their campfires.

13

How NOT to Choose a Campsite and then, What to do About it

When you find your site, the last available, you see that there is one little thing, your first challenge:

The campsite is not level.

In fact it is more than not level, it is seriously unlevel. It is pointing in a noticeably downhill direction. It has gouges and gullies where water likes to go ... a lot. You have images of rolling oranges, spiraling pasta, sliding plates, and difficulty rising in the morning due to loss of blood to the brain.

Perhaps this is why everyone around you made sure to get here earlier. There are actual differences in campsites. What a concept.

But wait. This is no time to shy away, to turn tail and run, this is a job for … manually adjusting hydraulic jacks! Just hope there's an uplifting moment in your immediate future.

Yes, these behemoths come with a jack system that raises the coach right up into the air so they hover like mastodons mid-jump. It's a little unsettling at first to walk by a motor home aloft but the consequences of not leveling the coach can be much worse than that nagging fear of instability. Most motor homes have refrigerators that will run your life by which I mean that, like an artful shrew, they will tyrannize the entire household with their fussy preferences. No refrigerator likes to be off-balance, and the kind I had was especially keen on remaining level fore to aft.

So there really wasn't any choice on that first night; if I wanted to stay at Camp Kitchegoomie, I had to level my rig because I had the last spot and my fridge did not like the site of it.

It may not seem like much to flip a few levers to get the motor home on an even keel, but together with all the other things I didn't know how to do yet, it was a little intimidating. I had experimented with the jacks before, but not with the refrigerator running and making audible demands.

The most daunting aspect of this project was the knowledge that I could do real damage to the motor home. You see, if you don't adjust the thing gradually and in the recommended order of steps, you can end up twisting the frame beyond repair.

Now, ask me what the proper order is. Well, I don't remember. And I don't remember because it wasn't written in any of the documentation I possessed — it had probably been lost — and I never wrote it down once I learned it. Just find out before you do it. Or get a new motor home, one that self-levels automatically.

So, my first surprise: after toggling on the power, the red and green lights on the console told me that one of the jacks was already slightly deployed (who knew?) below the chassis, kind of like driving around showing your underslip. Oops. I could have taken a stand on something long before I intended to.

When I pushed the first two levers I knew we were in for a ride. The jack motors whined and jerked and I could feel each little piston drop into position. Then there was a jolt and a quiver like a minor temblor and the whole front end of the coach started rising up into the air. This was like sitting in a on a magic carpet going up for a brake-job.

Speaking of which, you may ask, "You set the emergency brake ... didn't you?" Well, yes, what if I hadn't? Would the thing have backed, uninvited, into the cookout of the campers behind me? Maybe. Maybe not. And this is one of the wonders of RV camping. There are probably many hazardous consequences of an omission like that but for some reason the consequences just don't happen that often.

Every day, forgetful and negligent RVers are rewarded by the failure of terrible things to happen. Sometimes I'm not sure if this is a good thing or a bad thing.

So, with the coach set securely in place, what next? Jump enthusiastically out of the side door and look around for cheers and encouragement. Settle for a few half-hearted nods. Then unlock the drawer full of sewer equipment and survey the situation.

14

The Poop on, Well ... How NOT to Hold it

Why is it that the first thing people ask about RVing often has to do with poop? I can't quite figure it out, but for some reason friends and novices are preoccupied with the disposition of and contamination by poop while RVing. Common questions are, "Is it really disgusting to deal with the sewer stuff?" or, "So, do you have to empty the tanks often?" or "Does the sewage really smell in the motor home?" For some reason, it's hard to put folks at ease on this particular subject.

I have friends who have told me that it would take days before they would be willing to use the toilet in a motor home. I have to admit that although I was easily willing to pee in the bathroom, it took me a while to get comfortable putting

#2 in there. Is it because we are afraid we will be stuck with it? That we can't get it out of the coach once we put it in? Are we afraid that the movement of the coach will throw it back up into our living space? Is it that our incomplete evacuation demonstrates the failure of potty training, evoking deeply entrenched guilt and shame?

Ladies and gentlemen, I just don't know. But please, get over yourselves early, because carrying a toilet around with you can truly be a pleasure. Just think, as long as you've got your RV with you, never will you have to Hold It in a strange place while you find a bathroom that is always a few blocks farther than you thought. And never will you have to wonder who's been there just before you and what they were doing in there. As long as you stay close to the mother ship – and RVers do love to stay close to the mother ship – you can take your ease.

Yes, there is technique to it, knowledge that makes the difference between a foul-smelling hardened mass in your pipes and the free-flowing operation of a well-treated septic system, the zenith of convenience. But don't let me scare you. You can easily learn the difference.

But here's how NOT to use and maintain the coach's septic system:

First, keep a nice tight grip on your wallet and really stint on equipment and tank additives. That way, everything else will be tight – the hose, the tanks, and your gut, when they all get good and gummed up.

Here's what I mean. Reuse your sewer hose until the inside is so encrusted that you can't see the plastic sides or it just wears through with use. Picture where you will be and what you will be doing when the child from the next campsite runs over your worn hose with his bike, spraying sewage in a focused and forceful arc through your open window.

When you wash the hose after use by filling it partway with water, make sure that, in your panicky, neurotic attempt to rid yourself of its contents, that you swish it around so vigorously that you fling excrement onto the shoes of your horrified neighbor. (No, it was my neighbor who did that.)

Be stingy with the holding tank deodorant and, despite the instructions, add it before you've added the fresh water to the coach tanks. That way the green (or sometimes blue) stuff will clean only the short section of pipe way downstream below the tank, putting you up that creek we hear so much about. The green stuff you pour into your sewage tank (or black tank, as it's called) is designed to mix with the motion of the coach and break down solids. Any way you devise to inhibit that will make for really sludgy results.

Another sure technique for preventing the tank additive from working is, of course, to forget to add it at all, or, failing that, forgetting or refusing to add enough water to the tank as you go along. It will be very tempting to save water and therefore room in the tank so as to be able to boondock (dry camp without hook-ups) in the wilderness – or, if you prefer, the parking lot of some big box store – for longer without dumping. But again, think of the hardening mass. All you need is a little blockage and you have a constipated pachyderm on your hands who will require some serious ministrations.

There's special toilet paper you should use, too. How NOT to do it would be to use that cushy stuff you use at home, instead. The pleasure will be short-lived. And think of the damage you can do by stuffing tampons and chicken bones in the toilet because the green stuff doesn't work on any-thing but paper and what came out of you.

Need I say? How to DO it would be to use enough water to flush (read the instructions), pour in the tank chemicals AFTER you've run about 2 gallons into the tanks, and keep your sewer hose in good shape.

One of the frustrations of RVing is that your grey tank (wash-water) will always fill up before your black tank (sewer) does. For some reason, many motor homes are manufactured with grey and black tanks of equal size. Household water runs quickly, especially if you're showering so, to save room in the tank, some people dump what-ever they ethically can in the underbrush. What qualifies for this disposal method is leftover water in the drinking glasses or what's in the pot after steaming your green beans. Often, people use bio-degradable dishwashing soap and a plastic tub in the kitchen sink to catch rinse-water and dump it outside.

BUT IF YOU WANT TO REALLY SCREW UP, MAKE SURE TO DUMP IN THE WALMART PARKING LOT.

Leave NO TRACE in those parking lots, and leave only a minor trace in the woods and only if the trace is mostly water.

Now. Where was I? Oh.

15

How TO Spend Your First Night Away from Home

Here's what you *really* do. Turn on the propane and make yourself a nice dinner. Have a beer or a glass of wine. Write some notes about the events of the day and reflect on how fortunate you are. You have recognized something that few people do, that you are in the driver's seat. You have opened the landscape of your life in front of you and have set yourself in motion with new hope and curiosity. The fragrance of the world is sweeter, the colors brighter. Is it fear or excitement? Yes.

Go for a turn around the campground. This is your new community and most people have a lot more experience RVing than you do. If you feel like it, chat up a few folks, ask directions you don't need, listen to their stories. You might learn something.

You'll find most experienced RVers somewhat reluctant to charge right in with advice without being asked and this is partly because one source of amusement for them is the fumblings of the newbies. Some old hands can't resist the entertainment of a novice trying to connect the wrong hose to the water line, failing to engage the parking brake, or driving off with the awnings open. But if you ask for advice, or even if you don't, they are almost always happy to help and this is where you learn the best lessons of RVing and that you are not alone.

After your tour, brush your teeth, wash your face, and get in bed. Sneak the curtains open a little so you can see the moon, and lift the lid on your ceiling fan.

Let the cool evening air cascade onto your bare skin. Listen to the murmuring of the other campers around their campfires and the dog snuffling in the garbage. Sleep well my little hero, you have done a great thing.

16

How NOT to Entertain the Other Campers

The next morning you will find that a few coaches have already left the campground. Older people have an unmatched sense of urgency about RVing that propels them out of bed and onto the road before daybreak. Chances are you've heard a few bumps and scrapes, some hushed reproaches, and the rasp of a diesel pusher. But you're in no hurry. You've got the whole day ahead of you. Besides, you've accomplished something much bigger than you realize, your first day and night on the road.

Check the list once for breaking camp: disconnect and rinse the sewer line, unplug from shore power and water, turn off the propane, stow all the pots and pans, and close all the windows and fan lids. Check your oil, and check the Toad to make sure no one disengaged the hitch just for fun. Then get in the driver's seat, put on your pointless seat belt ...

and drive right off your hydraulic jacks, landing with a loud, bone-shaking thud on your front, unrecharged air-suspension.

Freeze. First hope that you haven't ruined the apple of your eye. Then hope that no one witnessed your stupid stupid stupid mistake. Look furtively out the windows. Then sneak out of the motor home and examine the front end as though you knew what you were looking for. The amazing thing: everything seems fine. It turns out that the jacks are designed to retract with any forward movement! Possibly, you are not the first person to accomplish this maneuver.

Although I didn't hear any suppressed laughter that morning, I am sure that a few campers told this story over the course of that day. But the forgiveness in this community is great because RVers are a relaxed, philosophical, and fun-loving lot. I have come to know that if something had gone really wrong, a throng would have been there to

help me. But as it was, I was grateful for the ano-
nymity of my leave-taking then.

The rest of the day proceeds without incident,
unless, of course, you count the exaltation of feeling that if you can survive such an error, the road
is yours. Set your course but don't get too attached
to it. A lot can happen in a day.

17

A Little Zap'll Do Ya (yes, this lesson is confusing)

OK. I suspect you're ready for the first mental challenge of this book. Don't be afraid if the technicalities don't make sense to you because you don't really have to understand it all. I'm telling you anyway, though, so you can pretend to see why something went wrong if it does go wrong.

If you think you don't understand how electricity works, wait until you buy an RV. Then you will *really* not understand how electricity works.

I recommend bringing a lot of sophisticated electronic equipment on a trip in a carbureted vehicle. Not that the carburetion interferes with the electricity, it's just an indication of how little your new home is prepared for what you probably intend to do in it.

What complicates the electrical situation is that your new household might be set up on 30- instead of 50-amp service. Now, you could avoid this by buying a vehicle with at least 50-amp service, but then you would miss all the fun of running a misfiring generator in order to have air conditioning or of limiting your travel to cool climates, praying (if you're me) that you never have to wear shorts to preserve brain function.

In the old days, people just sweated it out. No one expected to be as comfortable as we are today. Drivers just burned through one undershirt after another ... well, maybe that's just a stereotype.

And no one expected to be in constant communication – by cell phone, by email – in fact, no one *wanted* to be in constant communication because they wanted to get as far away as possible. Many of us may be missing the point of RVing but it's a fact that most of us now expect to have our fingers on the pulse of everyone's whatever. And theirs on yours. But in order to do that you will have to learn a little more about electricity than you probably know now.

The key is, never expect anything to work in a straightforward way. To start with, you may have to acquaint yourself with the converter that conditions electricity from an impolite form of DC (direct current) to a more refined, polite form of DC. You see, the coach has at least two forms of electricity, 110 AC and 12-volt DC, and depending on what you're trying to do you have to convert it or invert it first. The good news is that the converters and inverters are usually where they belong, in your RV and in your electronics, and do this automatically. The bad news is that if something stops working the garage guy will ask you where your converter is.

For related reasons, some equipment can be used sometimes and other equipment must be used other times. If you try to read by the light of the nifty spotlights mounted along the underside of the overhead cabinetry, your book will get dimmer and dimmer very quickly … if you are parked and you are not plugged in to shore power. That's because these require more power and are designed to be used when you're plugged in to AC.

On the other hand, if you try to read by the light of the hideous DC lamps hung over the dinette and kitchenette, your book will get dimmer more slowly ... if you are unplugged. That's because these draw less energy and can run off the battery longer.

If you want to read by the light of the one conventional reading lamp installed over the sofa, your book will blink on and off due to the intermittent short in the wiring.

If you want to listen to the radio while lying in your huge bed at the other end of the coach, you can do this using your handy dandy remote control. Yes, this is one of the few uncomplicated electrical pleasures of motor home life. If you installed it. Of course, you may have to get up to turn the thing off because the remote got a little damp.

Needless to say, there are multiple sources of power in the coach, each of which requires different kinds of fuel, and each of which can be variously transformed – or not – into different types of electricity, each of which, in turn, can be used in differing and limited ways:

- There's the generator that runs on gas and can recharge the engine battery but not necessarily the coach batteries. Oh. Did I mention there are two sets of batteries? One for the engine, usually two for the home? And a kill-switch that disconnects the engine from the engine battery and possibly another kill switch that disconnects the engine battery from the coach batteries?

- There's the engine that can recharge the batteries but only if they're connected in series.

- And there's the propane tank that powers your range and, under some conditions, your refrigerator, depending on whether electricity to the fridge is on or off …

But you shouldn't leave the propane on while you're driving (this is an important HOW TO, BTW).

And remember, it's fun to keep the number and location of fuse boxes a secret. From yourself. That way, when your windshield wipers quit – when it's raining – your search for the box and the replacement fuse can be edged with panic.

Actually, the fuse box for systems relating to vehicular functions was pretty easy to find. It was the breaker for the domestic functions that took me about three hours to find over the course of several days because I couldn't locate it in any of the original manuals. The previous owners had put it somewhere new! This, of course, is another advantage to buying an old vehicle: you know someone ran into some of the same problems you will encounter and did a retrofit; you often don't know how he or she solved the problem or where he or she put the thing or whether you're just too dumb to know what you're looking at.

(A prime example: I discovered a safe thoughtfully installed under the carpet in the bottom of the closet ... after I had thoughtfully installed a safe under a twin bed in the back. What's an extra 75 lbs of ballast? A lot. Did I ever use either safe? No. Too hard to reach.)

Actually, it's all really not that bad. There's one engine, one generator, one engine battery, at least two coach batteries (running the domestic functions), two kill switches, one converter, and three fuse boxes. There are monitors for most of these systems strewn around the the vehicle, some of which are not working because their lights have burned out. And then there's the extra inverter that you may or may not have brought for any special after-market electronics ... and all that cabling and antennae for the new am / fm / shortwave / broadband / telepathy weather radio, satellite Internet and TV (which I didn't have), and cell phone, each of the antennae requiring external mounts if you're driving an aluminum can.

Did I mention there's a water pump that should be on sometimes and DEFINITELY NOT ON other times?

There. I have conveyed the experience of total bewilderment.

18

Speaking of Electricity, Your RV is a Haven

It probably sounds as though, with a little bad luck, all your electrical systems are going to fail when you least expect it. Actually, not so much. Despite the fact that my Airstream needed some work, it amazed me with it's hardy, resilient design. It had some redundancy built in.

RVs are equipped with so many systems so you'll have plenty of options. For example, the AC and DC electrical systems make it possible for you to live in comfort whether you're plugged in at a lush RV resort in California or you're boondocking on a friend's back 40. Here's what I mean:

As I said, the refrigerator usually runs on three different kinds of power – shore power (meaning

AC, when you're plugged in at a campground); electricity generated by the engine of the RV when you're running it, (DC, civilized to 12-volt); and propane, which is easily refilled at many gas stations or campgrounds. So chances are that wherever you are, as long as you're not also sitting in the driver's seat, you can reach into the refrigerator and get a cold one, whatever that is to you. It also means that if one of these power sources fails you can use a back-up system.

Most RVs allow you, whether you're in line for a car ferry in Washington State or down an alley in Newburyport, to make a complete meal on your propane gas stove, take a shower using power from the domestic batteries, and listen to your favorite radio station while you're doing it. You just can't do all these things simultaneously for hours at a time. You have to be, shall we say, efficient.

I had a solar panel installed on my roof to help keep the batteries topped up when they weren't in use. How NOT to do it would be to allow the panels to get encrusted with bird poop, pine tar, and dust, and then wonder why you're not getting the juice you expect.

So despite some of the cautionary tales you read in this book, be reassured that usually the core domestic functions – electricity, water, sewage, and the kitchen appliances – work reliably no matter where you are. They're tough. When it starts to rain, you won't have to pitch a tent or find a cab or catch the right bus because it is not raining on you, the bugs are not coming through incompletely closed flaps, you can turn on the heat and you can cook a 5-course meal and invite the folks in the tent down the way.

It's nice to have something like that to offer, isn't it?

19

How NOT to Get On the Road in Earnest (actually, too bad Ernest didn't come)

I'm not going to tell you about the uneventful days – not that there are so many of them – because most RVers will regale you with stories about their nights on starry beaches, ice cream socials at their favorite campground, and they'll even complain a little. What they probably won't tell you is the stories in which they don't look too smart.

I had just been listening to an audiobook by a guy who traveled the world on a motorcycle, broke down many times, and lived to tell his tale. Then, all of a sudden, my coach started to lose power. Naturally, I thought my foot had slipped, so I gave her a little more gas. When she lost more power,

I thought maybe the engine was flooding and I took my foot off the gas. This worked for a minute but as soon as I put my foot back on the accelerator she hesitated again. And again. And again. And soon the lights on the dash came on and I was stalling downhill at 66 miles an hour with no power steering, standing on the brake.

What I had was vapor lock, which is vaporization of fuel in the fuel line, making it unpumpable by the fuel pumps. By the side of the road, I became convinced that the term vapor lock also refers to the trap in which you'll find yourself on the shoulder of some humid highway making a 3-hour tuna fish sandwich.

Predictably, vapor lock has the feature of tending to happen when you most need power, like when you're joining the traffic on the interstate or on a long, hard pull up the grade … in the rain … at the end of the day … when you're not sure where the campground is … and there's very little firm shoulder to pull onto.

Don't get me wrong, vapor lock can also happen in lovely, undulating farmland dotted with tidy homes, in a gas station where there are plenty of services, in front of a café with wifi or down the street from a cute B&B. But does it usually happen there? Noooooooooo.

I had heard before I bought this coach that vapor lock plagued this particular model so I took what measures I could and figured the Mini would save me from the worst. I installed a new exhaust system that would disperse more heat, I increased the insulation on the gas line that paralleled the exhaust pipe, thereby minimizing heat we couldn't eliminate. But the 1986 Airstream 345 motor home had a design flaw, probably as a lesson in existential equanimity. And who knows, Airstream probably had a point. (To be fair, since then they changed their minds and make motor homes without the vapor lock option.)

On this day, vapor lock happened on an anonymous stretch of interstate, far from the nearest exit, at the end of a long, hot drive in the Appalachian Mountains. Thank God, I said to myself, for the Mini. When the coach engine still didn't restart after an hour and a half, I got out of the motor home and unhitched the Mini, congratulating myself on my providence. I got in the car and turned the key. And of course, the engine would not start.

Did you remember that you have to recharge the battery of your Toad while driving because the auxiliary braking system runs it down? Nooooooooooo.

Back into the coach to regroup.

Have you ever stood by the side of a highway or attempted to relax in a motor home adjacent to high-speed traffic? Picture this: you are just sitting down to a deliberately made tuna fish sandwich with all the trimmings and suddenly your world is distorted by a huge, braying monster on the street-side. This is the action of a big rig, those out-size cattle of the road which, if you're lucky, are driven by skilled, considerate, experienced operators who will teach you a lot about how to conduct yourself as the driver of a rig of your own, but who, if you're unlucky, will get away with every last inch on the highway, intimidating everyone within a 15-foot radius. In the case of a pretty big motor home on the shoulder, truckers may have little choice if they're boxed in on their left. When they push through the gap, the vacuum created between two long vehicles is considerable and can leave you with a flip in your street-side hairdo.

It is for this, among many, reasons that state troopers do not encourage lollygagging by the side of the road. They will politely and circumspectly investigate all RVs on the shoulder, expecting to find heart-attack victims or drivers so demented they've forgotten the names of their co-pilots. They will also prompt a mentally competent driver to get off the shoulder quickly. So it really isn't a good option (and it's not safe anyway) to camp for too long on the shoulder.

Consequently, I had a double-tow on my hands. And if you think you can call Joe's Ad Hoc Garage down the street for this expedition, you will be sorely disappointed.

20

How NOT to Offend the Knight in Shining Armor

I don't know how often customers genuflect to Good Sam's tow-truck drivers, but it probably doesn't hurt. Here's what you do when a man with a broad West Virginian accent and a twinkle in his eye picks you up with your two hot but unresponsive vehicles:

Get off your knees, offer him your Good Sam ID card and pretend you know what you're talking about. Tell him the coach is vapor-locked and the Mini is mysteriously out of commission. Do not tell him that you didn't remember you had to recharge your Toad. You are not fooling anyone, but at least you maintain some dignity.

Then obediently get in the passenger seat of his oil-soaked tow-truck and hope he's not an ax-murderer. After many such towing experiences, I've found that ax-murderers are uncommon among this breed of mostly good-natured, seen-it-all tradesmen.

That's how I spent a couple of days at the Ramada Inn in Appalachia. They ordered a part that was helpful but turned out to be unrelated to the cause of the problem. It was there that I learned exactly what is necessary to run the engine of the Toad *while I am towing it* in order to recharge the battery for use with the auxiliary brakes.

There are plenty of things you'll forget when you start. They tend not to kill you.

21

How NOT to Save Fuel

I know people complain about how much gas those big ole motor homes consume. But really, they don't know the half of it.

Here's how to consume as much gas as possible in a short period of time. First, notice that if you have a vintage motor home it will only cool you if you run the generator. Attempt to convince yourself first that the dash a/c is adequate. Turn up the fan speed in the cab console as high as you can and bask in the loud noise.

Then, opt for a bigger breeze and open all the windows while trying to listen to the radio. Pull down all the windshield flaps and draw the side curtains so as to shut out as much light, heat – oh, and visibility – as possible. Hold the driver's side curtain in your left hand because the draft from the window wants to suck it out. Tell yourself this is safe because the road is straight and nothing much is going to happen.

All right, get real. Pull over. It's time to start the generator because this is the only source of power great enough to run the air conditioners thoughtfully installed in the roof.

There are two air conditioners but the generator will only run one at a time (Everyone up front!) To start the generator, put your finger on the toggle switch and then feel the entire motor home lurch, buck, and growl so loudly that you are convinced you've wakened a beast of legends untold. But it's just that the generator is not firing evenly and probably therefore stinks. Oops. We forgot to tune it up. Oh well. No one will hear and smell it but you … and any driver who passes and any pedestrian with lousy luck.

Pretend that you have adequately cleaned the filters on the air conditioners and that the forks you have used to prop open the a/c louvers will not take a bite out of you in the event of high-speed impact.

Get back in the driver's seat and feel the arctic air on your right shoulder blade. The unit is noisy but effective and definitely an improvement. Rejoin traffic and take stock.

Here's the situation. You are now driving a vehicle with two thirsty engines running. But that's not all. Recall that in order to run the auxiliary braking system the Toad battery has to be recharged periodically. What this means is that *every 2.5 hours or so you have to stop the coach, get into the Toad, and start the Toad's engine.*

Now picture this, you are driving through a quiet, conventional, modest-sized town in a pretty unusual rig, with the engine running, the generator running for the a/c, the Toad engine running, and, yes, even the fan in the Toad engine running to keep the Toad engine cool. You are sucking some serious petroleum.

But that's only the immoral part.

Now, think about it again: you will have to stop for gas even sooner because you are now burning fuel at a much higher rate. The fact that it is a hot day means that you are especially subject to vapor lock. This means that you cannot pause for long anywhere because the heat has a way of building in the lines (rather than being cooled by the moving air), thus vaporizing the fuel.

Also, consider that, as has been necessary all through the trip, you still want to keep the motor home gas tanks partially empty at all times to avoid straining the engine with unnecessary weight on steep grades (a small price to pay for the heavier Toad you fell in love with, remember?) Therefore, you have to stop for gas even more frequently. And that means there will be many more opportunities for vapor lock to develop at all the stops at the gas stations ... when the heat builds up in your fuel line (didn't I warn you?) and vaporizes the fuel while you are paused at a stop to refuel.

So how do you time the various stops – to gas up, to start the Toad engine, to shut off the Toad engine – without getting stuck in the middle of traffic somewhere with vapor lock and three motors running? You can't really, you just do a lot of running around – in and out of the motor home, the

Toad, the gas station, the Toad, the motor home, the Toad – and you try to do it where you're willing to make a 3-hour, tunafish sandwich.

If you're driving an old rig that gets vapor lock, I recommend that you have a lot of time on your hands. Or a life-time, free-tow deal with Good Sam.

22

How NOT to Save Money

I am not simply a gas-hog RV driver. I have another side. I am a sucker. And one of the things I am a sucker for is ways to prevent offense if I possibly can.

So, because I believed that a generator is inherently stinky and that I'd have to be using it in the campground, I was determined to minimize its obnoxious effects. To do this, I bought a generator chimney at an RV rally which is RV Sucker Heaven.

Now, a generator chimney is a good idea. It sticks right up the side of the motor home and redirects the exhaust and some of the noise up and over. It stores neatly in an outer bay and is easily assembled and mounted for use. I pictured par-rying all kinds of complaints from campground neighbors when running the air conditioning.

There was just one problem that I discovered later. Most campgrounds don't allow the use of generators any more. And the other times you'd use the generator tend to be those in which you are not surrounded by human neighbors. I sup-pose someone could have pointed that out. But why interrupt a New Yorker with her wallet out?

And that's not all I fell for.

At that very same RV show, I came upon a booth where they were selling the perfect solution to the problem of Odor Backwash. Mind you, I have never had the problem of Odor Backwash (in which the sewer tank smells emitting from the roof vent wash back into the windows of the motor home). Odor Backwash may well reside in the minds of People Preoccupied with Poop.

So, since of course I was not one of those peo-ple but wanted to protect those people, I bought one. It's a fin-like plastic thing that fits on the top of your vent pipe. Never mind that it's designed for the big, square, white motor homes and not for a curved aluminum skin. But I felt better knowing I had it, and it's still sitting under my couch in the motor home in case of Sudden Odor Backwash.

23

How NOT to Know Your Limits

Seriously, are you someone who is going to check the charge of your batteries? Because if you are, you need a hydrometer, a special gauge for judging specific gravity. I, of course, bought one.

Are you someone who is going to lubricate every moving part yourself? Because if you are, you need about 5 different lubricants, each uniquely suited to its function. Avoid WD-40 because it absorbs dirt, paraffin is for the stairs, don't use oil that's too light on parts that undergo a lot of friction. I, of course, have every one of these lubricants. In fact, I still have almost as much of those lubricants as I did when I left Connecticut. Thank God the motyho is an Airstream.

Are you going to prevent all foreign objects, including rain, from adhering to the windows of the coach? The truckers do it. Sounds like a good idea, too, huh? And it really works. So go ahead and buy multiple bottles of Rain-X that requires each glass surface to be prohibitively clean. I've preserved my ample supply of Rain-X too.

Are you going to buff and shine every aluminum surface and crevice to restore it to its factory-fresh finish? Because if you are, you should stock up on all of the products specific to the maintenance of aluminum with a Clear Coat seal. Don't just put any old polish on it because you might end up with psoriasis of the coach – which I have witnessed. Some of these products weigh a lot. You can still see a slight sag under the sink in my motor home ... because they are still on that shelf.

And are you going to stage a solo, virtuoso performance in a dark place like a forest? Then make sure you replace the broken swiveling spotlight on the roof of your vehicle to the tune of a couple of hundred dollars. Otherwise, I'd forget it.

Get the idea?

Choose your battles, and for the stuff you aren't going to do yourself, trade your cooking or story-telling or Internet skills for what someone in the campground can do for you. There's no reason you have to do it all yourself.

24

A Day in the Life of a Driver of an Elderly Vehicle

So you're battling vapor lock on a rainy stretch of road in Illinois. You've developed a technique for feeding her a little gas until just before she stalls and then coasting as far as you can get away with it. This all seems like a pretty good idea, especially since you know that campground has got to be around here somewhere, but suddenly getting off the highway gets a little more complicated.

In your attempt to change lanes to get onto the shoulder, you've discovered that the signal isn't getting out. In fact, there is no signal at all, it's broken. That you are trying to move to the right makes matters worse because you can barely see to the right under the best of conditions. Realize quickly that in order for vehicles behind you to see your arm gestures indicating a lane change to the right, you have to pull briefly left so that your arm is visible beyond the length of the coach. Then you have to pull right again to change to the right-most lane and you have to do this without fishtailing.

Here's the stop-gap solution. Once safely by the side of the road, dig out your two-foot window squeegee and clothe it in your brightest, reddest turtleneck sweater. Make sure the sleeves move freely so that it looks like a flailing hostage. When necessary, shove the thing out the window – up for right turns, left for left turns – and hold on for dear life lest the wind rip it out of your hands. Oh. Maintain control of your 50-foot-rig with the other hand.

If this isn't absurd enough wait until you're back on the road the next day. Pull into a Flying J to make lunch. Just park out in the big-rig spaces as you usually do and then try to get out of the coach for some supplies. Press the door latch. Press it again. Throw your weight against the door in case it's just jammed. Find that you are locked in.

Review the pros and cons of climbing out the back where the emergency window is. You scraped your thigh the last time you tried that when you and the RV salesman got trapped inside on the sales lot. Open the side window and start yelling. Wave. Laugh. Say please. Beg repeatedly. Bang on the side of the coach.

When no one bothers to acknowledge you, start up the engine and drive right up to the pumps and block as many of them as you can. More calls for help may finally attract the attention of a stout, bored woman who will open your door.

Well, I guess not all drivers are a relaxed, philosophical, and fun-loving lot.

Once back on the interstate, driving without signals, waving your red, inflated squeegee doll and, waiting for the next stall, watch the door unexpectedly blow open despite the elaborate cat's cradle of string you'd used to fasten it at the truck stop. Decide it is time for a trip to Airstream.

25

How NOT to Entertain the Manufacturers

So that's how I ended up camped out in front of the Airstream factory for a week waiting for an appointment.

It's not that I hadn't intended to go to the Airstream factory. For most Airstream owners it's a pilgrimage. There really is something special about their product and it starts with the appearance of the thing and what it conjures of the early space age and mid-20th-century courage of an America ready to tackle anything. The new trailers are state-of-the-art design. I don't mean amenities; anybody can put a woodstove or a big tub in a motor home. But not everyone can design a vehicle that makes you feel special and a part of something transcendent and rewards you in every corner with an elegant solution to common design problems.

There's a lot of respect in the Airstream community for the older vehicles. Many of the architectural challenges were solved early on and their trailers have a reputation for enduring for decades and maintaining much of their value. Some people like to shine the old ones to a blinding mirror finish that, yes, has probably caused vehicular accidents. But those trailers are a delight to behold.

My coach, on the other hand, was not in top shape when I bought her. She was almost vintage after all, and you really have to stay on top of the details of something as big and as complex as these vehicles are. Imagine that you sliced your apartment away from the rest of the building and put it on a flat bed and started driving. The problems you'd run into are not far from the ones occurring in the average motor home; it's amazing these coaches hang together as well as they do. And for a vehicle her age, mine is in remarkably good condition.

As it turns out, my stay at Airstream was one of the most pleasant weeks of my trip. It was a creative time because I knew I was in a good place where they'd take care of me and I could concentrate on my work. There was something very peaceful about camping in Airstream's Terraport watching the cows graze in nearby fields and the huge sky of white and grey elephants heading eastward. I suppose I could have taken their direction as a hint to quit while I was ahead, but Airstream Inc. wouldn't have wanted to miss the chance to make a little money off of my insurance company. And I knew I was in the only hands that could help.

There's a little story I haven't told you that had already put this trip to Airstream on the list of things to do. It's the kind of experience that is key to impressing tradesmen that you are a skilled, if new, motor home driver. I figured this out back in Connecticut when I was readying for the trip and went to have new carpet installed throughout the coach.

I was proud of my skills and had the reputation among friends and family of being a very competent driver, one willing and able to tackle ambitious tasks – like driving trucks and buses and motor homes towing Mini Coopers. It was always me, after all, whom friends and family might ask to do the parallel parking in an unusually tight squeeze. So it was with a certain amount of bravado that I had gone for my third trip in the motor home to the carpet store and left her there for the work.

So here's my advice on how NOT to get the biggest bang for your carpet buck: Arrive early to inspect all the work they've done, ask all the right questions about aspects of the work – were there any remnants? Did they also manage to fit it under the benches and neatly around the doghouse covering the engine? – Pay them a lot of money and thank them for their prompt and skillful completion of the job.

Then get in the coach, maneuver her skillfully around a number of obstacles in the back parking lot, slip her through the narrow side alley, and then up under the eaves of their storage shed, lifting the roof every so slightly, shaving the fascia board off the front and creating several long, ugly, and very expensive creases in the apple of your eye.

You'll soon note that you can move neither forward nor backward without destroying more. Sit at the wheel as workmen and horrified but amused onlookers inspect the damage. Then wait for someone to borrow a forklift to raise the roof of the building to free you. Did I mention that this should be on a Friday evening when everyone wants to go home?

So I had many motives for my trip to Airstream, one of the biggest being that I was about to make a huge claim on my insurance. If you think the dealer in Connecticut had been glad to see me …

About $15,000 worth of repairs later I was back on the road.

This is when I am glad you are reading this at your place and not here laughing at me.

26

How NOT to Shower in a Motor Home

If you hang around for a while in a very busy campground or you boondock in a sylvan glade with no services, sooner or later you will want to take a shower. Did I explain about the shower?

In my coach, showering is a pleasure. For one thing, it's cozy. Your aluminum shell has that rounded fuselage-type design with implications for internal space usage. Wonder of wonders, there's a specially sculpted shower cabinet made to fit the contours.

If you're tall, what that means is you're a little stooped in the shower unless you like sitting on the custom sculpted shower seat which, to me, is a real luxury. When I looked in the shower in the Airstream for the first time, I said, "A seat!" I didn't say, "How do I stand up straight?"

I've always loved sitting in a shower but seating is rarely provided. In the Airstream the way they've worked it is that heating of various kinds runs under the bench so that when you sit down it's already kinda toasty and then you can shave your legs or serve tea, whatever you had in mind.

The shower is also a good place for storing things that spill while in transit. It's a good place for tossing big suitcases. And it's a good place to find dirty water up to your ankles.

How does this happen, you may ask?

Well, the filling and draining of waste tanks is a rhythm of life that you'll have to learn. You see, it's not really a great idea to just leave the tank valves open while you're hooked up to the campground sewer so that the waste runs directly from your fixtures and into the ground. That would be way too straightforward.

It's good to get some heavy volume going through the lines because volume is what keeps the lines clear. If you just have a little sludge drifting its way through the toilet drain on your occasional flushes it tends to dry up and clog the lines and valves. And waste from cooking, especially if you like those high-fat specials like deep fry and barbeque, is surprisingly adhesive because, as you might guess, it does the same thing to your pipes as it does to your dishes.

So what this means is that you're really better off keeping the valves to the sewer tank closed until it's almost full and then draining it all at once. It gives the green stuff a chance to work in the tank, breaking the sludge down and disinfecting it. Then it's good to have some volume in the grey tank to wash out the valve after you've emptied the black tank – the two tanks share a valve. You don't have to do this all the time with the grey tank water, just every now and then.

Here's how NOT to do it and get a dishwater pedicure:

Roll the dice. Don't bother to check the tank monitor on your control panel, just leave it to chance that you're going to have enough room in the grey tank to absorb the waste water from your shower. Sit down on the shower seat, turn on that warm, relaxing water, exult in the lavishness of it all – your own private space in a campground of moldy bathrooms teeming with children with behavior disorders – and soap up. Think about whether it actually might be nice to have a cup of tea while you're at it and then notice the water level rising. Notice it after you've shaved one leg and not the other.

I suppose it's not such a bad thing to towel the soap off and run outside in your bathrobe to drain the grey tank. But have you ever squatted under an old vehicle while wearing a white bathrobe with nothing on underneath? Not only are you likely to pick up something black and smudgy, but you are dangerously close to making some new friends.

Now, of course, the same vigilance about over-full tanks goes for the toilet. You were waiting for this, weren't you? To help you conserve room in the tank and insure Smooth Operation of All Things, the toilet comes with foot pedals. Don't bother to spend a lot of time sitting on the toilet and playing with the foot pedals. It's just not that rewarding, even though it's tempting for those of us who play the piano.

There may be two foot-pedals, or one that depresses half-way and then all the way; one pedal (or setting) adds water, and the other opens the valve to flush. The idea is that you add a little water before you poo, get the solids good and soupy before you flush it, and that you don't just let a lot of fresh water run down through the toilet as you empty it, especially if it's just #1.

In my coach there is a wand next to the toilet used for extreme cases. It's actually a rigid hose and, when hooked up to the water line – that you've disconnected from the commode for the purpose – can be squirted directly onto The Stuff You're Sending Elsewhere.

How NOT to do it would be to ignore the fact that you are living in a closed system that requires new skills. It won't be a closed system for long because you will overload it.

OK, I won't say anything more. In this section.

27

More Ways NOT to Entertain Other Campers

One way to entertain other campers – if it doesn't gross them out first – is to pull out of the camp-ground with the cap to your sewer tanks dangling from under the coach and a stream of material flowing from the mostly-empty reservoir because the internal valve is not so tight. Sure, you may hear a note of disapproval, but mostly they're happy knowing that you, too, have, at least once, forgotten to button your diaper.

It's also fun to pull away from the campsite without having disconnected the water hose or the electric cord. If you're lucky, this will result in both a geyser and a shower of sparks. Not the safest combination, but, as long as no one's hurt, good for a few laughs.

But my favorite way to entertain other campers would have to be: Prepare for take-off in the usual ways – unplug, close the awnings, turn off the propane, and shut all the windows. Batten everything down. Lock the door to the motor home, sit down in the driver's seat, put on your pointless seatbelt, and drive confidently toward the campground exit. Make sure you demonstrate your now-expert judgment of distances based on your intimate knowledge of the shape and size of the coach. Hear a sickening crunch and notice you're losing momentum on the curbside.

Run through the checklist in your mind. Then stop doing that because it's not going to help to be right. Get up and open the door to the motor home. Catch yourself before you fall directly into the dirt when your foot misses a step that is no longer there. Well, it is still there, twisted into your new spiral staircase leading directly under the motor home.

How does this happen? Because you didn't *really* hear the stairs retract. Stand by with embarrassment and abject gratitude while the really nice guy who can fix almost anything hammers the assembly back into good enough shape to allow you back into your home.

Can you tell which of these I did and which I did not do?

28

How NOT to Entertain Other Drivers

Once back on the road, you'll find numerous ways to entertain other drives. One way is to present a picture of obscurity while driving. How? Cover as much window as possible to limit the heat from the sun and wear a big floppy hat with lots of holes in it (for seeing) to protect your face from the heat and glare of the road. Watch the oncoming drivers do a double take when they see a Mexican cowboy asleep at the wheel. Perhaps it would be fairer to say that this is a way of entertaining yourself. But there are other ways to make other drivers laugh.

Begin a steep ascent knowing that your motor home will slow to 20 miles per hour and that it will stall from vapor lock if you stop. Of course, the other drivers won't know this and they will just honk and gesture vulgarly hoping to shame you to the side of the road – where you will have to spend the day. Although strictly speaking this is not entertaining to them, I suppose it could be diverting if you then got back on the road attempting to rejoin traffic and then stalled in the lane.

One of my absolute favorite methods is to set out on your trip without having locked the outer bay drawers. On most motor homes, drawers run the length of the coach and contain things like camping gear, extra paper towels and sewer equipment. In the right circumstances, having unlocked outer bay drawers results in a kind of jack-in-the-box effect in which the drawers slide open, widening your vehicle by a couple of feet on either side as you turn, in a kind of rhythm of the road, keeping the drivers in neighboring lanes guessing. This is a good way to discourage passing on a narrow stretch of construction and may appeal to people seeking to find their exploits on YouTube.

PART THREE

And Then There's the Journey

29

The Vehicle is Not the Trip

There are many days of driving, and, if you're not careful, too many hours of making and breaking camp. It's important to remember that you don't just drive in and out; there's a lot to do to camp in an RV responsibly, abiding by the rules of campground etiquette. You could pass with only minimal effort in a campsite but, really, most people make sure they're good neighbors – keeping the garbage under control, not allowing leaks from the water-hose, straightening up promptly after a barbeque – and all these things take time.

The real point is, if you're like me, you can easily let the comings and goings, the mechanics and the coach itself eclipse the journey, especially when you're so new to it all. I make no pretense here at Zen and the Art of RVing. I'm fighting unconsciousness daily just like the rest of you. Remember, this trip for me came under the heading: "physician heal thyself." My one stab at Zen wisdom is: don't spend too much time coming and going, spend a lot of time being, and then, when it's time to go, really go.

30

Dawn Procession

Some of the most glorious mornings on my trip were on the road at sunrise, ascending the High Plains toward the Rockies under a cloudless sky. But what made these mornings more glorious were the truckers.

Only truckers may appreciate this, but for some reason, at 5 a.m., a gleaming silver tanker with amber running lights stands out for what it is: a vision of strength and persistence, sexy and elegant. And for some, possibly similar reason, the rigs out at that time of the morning are some of the cleanest, best-kept rigs you will see on the road. Maybe it's because they're the only ones out at that hour so you get a better look at them, but I suspect that it's a self-selected group, long-haulers who have some experience and pride in what they do, who rise early because they're ready, and who prefer by now to avoid wallowing in the heat and traffic of the day.

It was an honor to join this majestic caravan of loners burning thousands of gallons of diesel fuel in the ill-conceived but still laudable task of spanning this huge, mostly uninhabited country. But it was an even greater honor when, repeatedly, the drivers of 50-foot Peterbilts, immaculate in their glazes of burgundy or hunter green, chrome shined to blinding, would flash their running lights and cock their driver's side hand low in their windscreen or out the side window to greet me.

But I guess it's not often you see a rig like mine, either.

There are many of us on the road; most of us are windshields to one another. When I was first learning to drive as a kid it took me a while to grasp that I should be communicating with the person behind the wheel in that other car rather than attempting to predict the actions of a large, cold, metal box.

I've found that the easiest way to talk to other drivers is with my arm out the window. In some parts of the world, usually the warmer ones, this technique is de rigueur. Of course, we can't always expose ourselves that way, but the nuances of expression will make up for a watch (if you still wear one) that doesn't run.

Some truckers are so accustomed to greeting one another that they've shortened the wave to a barely perceptible wrist rotation in the low, street-side corner of their windshield. Others nod. Some, if they are feeling expansive or grateful will flash their ICCs, the amber running lights. These are often reserved for Thank You signals to another trucker who, say, has let his colleague cut him off in the slow lane rather than forcing her to lose too much momentum in the fast lane on a steep grade.

But it's also a signal for you in the half-light when they like your rig.

31

Dust Thou Art, or How NOT to Join an Arts Movement

This is an adventure, right? So you're supposed to push the limits, really try stuff you've never tried before. Go ahead, let your hair down, go to Burning Man.

Now, I think Burning Man shows up on someone's list of 100 things you should do once before you die. I don't think it's insignificant that they say, "once" because the average person, having once thrust himself in, would discover it's somewhere he doesn't belong. But if you are artistic, the spirit of experimentation gets you there the first time, so I arranged with my sister to attend Burning Man, one of the major arts events of the

Western hemisphere, this annual convention of artists, would-be artists, and Imposters Like Me at a desert free-for-all of artwork, dust, and a moderate degree of debauchery.

Burning Man started as a courageous and innovative gathering in the San Francisco Bay Area, and, partly due to its mushrooming popularity, moved quickly to the Nevada desert for their annual Labor-Day-week festival restoring the arts to their rightful place in life. Burning Man gets its name from the culminating event in which a huge wooden man is set afire surrounded by pounding drums, music, and the inflamed psyches of thousands. It's quite a tribal experience even if it isn't your tribe.

The year I was there, 27,000 people transformed the dusty desert flatland into a throbbing mandala-shaped arts-organism, composed of concentric rings of campsites studded with 30-foot sculptures, soaring colorful tents, and crisscrossed by art-cars in the form of fire breathing dragons and other fantastic beasties. At the center of the camp was a tent offering minimal services and providing an opportunity for the gathering of bodies in varying degrees of relaxation, intersecting like free radicals bumping in the night.

Much of Burning Man is wondrous and exciting. In exchange for admittance, all they require (in addition to $400+) is that you participate in an artwork. Not too much to ask, right? The problem with Burning Man is that it has attracted many wannabes who have no real intention to contribute and instead lard up the week's creative outpouring that is, otherwise, a unique marvel of invention.

But if you find yourself on the road to Burning Man, burning with good intentions, here's how NOT to do it:

First, instead of in a coach full of party-happy creators, find yourself heading to the desert with your sister – to whom you have always been the soul of propriety – and just one other traveler whom you don't know well and who is also a psychotherapist.

It's fine if you want to carry with you everything you can possibly need for a week – you have to – but remember to bring along an incompletely conceived art-project doomed to failure. Make only a nod to the theme of that year's event – Theater of the Body – and load up the vehicle with boxes and boxes of surgical gloves and a single tank of helium for your installation, Hands Across the Desert. Or was it Lending a Hand? Or was it Let's Shake Hands? For some reason I can't get it straight.

Equip yourself with miles of silver ribbon that you have not tested as a closure for the gloves. Assure yourself that there will be no problem inflating thousands of gloves from the helium tank through the glove-sleeves and that there will be even less problem tying off the sleeves with slippery pieces of metallic ribbon. The idea is that you will string these floating hands that you will have sprayed with reflecting paint from your vehicle to all the neighboring vehicles. Forget to bring the reflecting paint.

Then get in the clean, well-cared for motor home that you have invested way too much after-market money in and drive her directly into the heat of the desert without having waxed her against sun and sand. Watch the temperature gauge climb and pray that you don't get vapor lock miles from the nearest phone or road. Smile wanly to your passengers and fuss unnecessarily about small things like whether someone's useless cellphone is plugged into the right electrical socket.

As you get closer to the site, notice that every one of the other vehicles is older, dirtier, or more covered with artwork than yours. Compare your 35-foot coach carrying three people to the 14-foot vehicles carrying 5, bulging with makeshift bags and tents. Feel like a spoiled idiot. Smile somewhat more genuinely as you approach the gate and see that you are not being greeted with derision.

When the bearded, skirted man working security asks whether he can climb on the roof to check for stowaways, consider your options: If you say no, you will forever humiliate your passengers and will be turned away at the door. If you say yes, a dent may be formed in the delicate skin of your motor home. Opt for the second alternative … and the resulting dent.

Then join the exuberant cheering and chanting at the entrance with the forced hilarity of the Republican Whip at a Log Cabin (Gay) Republican fundraiser. Drive through columns of attendees greeting participants from previous Burnings Man and soaking up all the available camping space. Then insinuate yourselves into a spot and notice your free-love neighbors eye you with suspicion and disappointment.

Watch your sister and her friend change into their Burning Man clothes. Realize that you haven't owned anything like Burning Man clothes in your entire life, let alone know how to compose a fetching ensemble. Tell them you don't really feel like going for a walk and take a nap instead.

By nightfall, your sister has returned with Reports From Afar and you are getting your second wind. As the sun sets marking the commencement of the evening's extravagant goings-on, hum weakly as the camp ululates to greet the night. Ransack your closet for something to pass as Burning Man Clothes and remember with relief that you, too, have brought some blinking, luminous gadgets.

One of the marvels of Burning Man is the transformation of the night. It is truly magical.

From all over the round camp emerge dancing figures etched and sculpted in light-wires, colored lights that can be bent and shaped to any desired form. With her foresight (and past experience) your sister has brought some blinking witches hats and glow-tubes that can be worn around the neck and arms. Layer them on, hoping no one notices your conventional attire. (Learn later that these devices are frowned upon for ecological reasons.)

Follow the crowds out into the open area to see the art installations. There are 30-foot castles made of sculpted, folded paper; rounded futuristic plastic chambers of light and sound; a 20-foot luminescent skull on wheels; and dozens of visual jokes motorized and not.

The desert literally pulses with sound; you can feel it in your tissues, as though a shared heart were bursting through your skin.

For a couple of hours you wander around and grab a ride on the occasional dragon which stalls for long periods of time while mechanics work on the machinery. When you tire of this, it's off to bed.

The next day or two pass similarly, with much lounging done around the motor home during the day. (Remember I said RVers like to stay close to the mother ship?) The sun is hot and most people sleep in after the night's revelries. Get up early because you keep forgetting to attend the night's revelries and entertain yourself by reading the New Yorker under the striped awnings and by trying to inflate the surgical gloves, to no avail. You have achieved only long strands of flaccid hands, dangling obscenely among local tent posts. It has become obvious quickly that you have bombed on the art part, all that's left is to try to mingle adequately with the crowds.

But there is another development. It's the dust. The motor home looks powdered, then generally lighter in color, then drifted, as the dust from the desert accumulates in every possible crevice. Your hair, unteased, takes on a consistency usually accomplished once a year at Halloween and only with hours of hairspray. Things taste gritty. Even the liberal use of water – a hoarded resource – only creates a paste.

You can't be sure exactly how all the days pass. Your photographs will be strangely timeless; only one thing, your hair, an expanding fright wig, marks the passage. Finally, on Saturday prepare to go. Wave goodbye to your neighbors, still as puzzled about you as when you arrived, and head back to civilization.

The most comfortable campground you can find nearby will be in Truckee, California. Boy, is it nice by comparison. It is entirely forested by a canopy of evergreen trees dwarfing the homes-on-wheels below. A couple of days will not be enough to clean the coach, it will take a full week to get the dust out because you didn't keep your windows shut. As you wax her, silently, repeatedly, apologize, "Never again." Promise. Don't go to Burning Man in a vehicle you care anything about. But give something like Burning Man a try. If Burning Man doesn't suit you, other experiments will.

32

The Mother Ship

By now, you've heard me refer to the RV as the Mother Ship twice. But twice is just the tip of the iceberg.

Observed from a distance, RVers are puzzling. They drive around the country in something As Close to Home as Possible. They've brought the same dishes, the same recipes, the same hobbies, the same TV habits. And most of them absorb little, stylistically, from their travels. They may collect decorative plates from Graceland, a straw hat from Mexico, and pack an assortment of regional seasonings, but in most cases, the RV that leaves home closely resembles the RV that returns.

At some campgrounds, the vehicles mass in tight packs in what looks more like a shopping mall parking lot than an outdoor experience. Sometimes there's not a tree in sight. On hot days, the occupants are likely to keep the windows tightly shut, the sunshades down, and to consume huge amounts of energy running ovens, TVs, multiple air conditioners and are throwing off a lot of heat doing it, so when the rare pedestrian passes by, it's even hotter, it's noisy, and it's forbidding. And as we all know anyway, one dare not knock on the door when the blue heart flickers from within.

Where is the charm in this, you may ask?

Well, I'm stumped. I hated those campgrounds and avoided them avidly. Also, in my old coach, I had plenty of fun with only a microwave and a/c I couldn't run without a prohibited generator. I was more than satisfied in a 35-foot vehicle and more living space than the average traveling family of four could afford, with a full kitchen and bathroom, central heat, and two striped awnings on either side of the vehicle. Not to mention a swiveling spotlight on top. Tough, huh?

But I believe I can answer why RVers do what they do. We are all performing experiments in change and discovering our own tolerance for uncertainty. For some people the challenge is, how far away from home can I go and still be comfortable? So we take little steps. We take most of home with us. Is it a bad thing that we are burning the same fuel on the road as we do at home? There may be no net environmental damage, depending on how far you drive, you could be using less. Do we owe it to anyone to do more than we do? And what are we interested in? Whether we feel good or not, whether we feel free, and perhaps whether we learn something or return instead a cowed, homesick, travel-failure.

To give up everything I knew, I had to take a lot of it with me. I had to carry my home on my back in order to feel safe leaving home. Yeah, it's not the most radical experiment, but I think it speaks to the question of why people like to stay close to the Mother Ship. Because, silly, she's the mother.

RVers will cover thousands of miles across unfamiliar terrain and outrun tornadoes but when it comes to dinner time, they may choose to sit right next to the ticking, cooling engine, break out a beer and huddle in the shadow of their Mother Beast when they could be 50 yards down the path at the beach or 5 miles down the road at a charming bistro on the water. It's because we all have our limits and sometimes home is just home, no matter whether it moves at 70 miles an hour or not.

And then there's the neighborhood. No, you can't have much of a conversation when you're locked up tight in your air-conditioned vehicle, but there are many times when a/c is not necessary. If the weather's temperate, most RVers will emerge from their locomotive castles and mark their 15-foot radius, set up their barbeques, and then walk their pets in the hopes of making an overture. Those without pets will borrow a spatula, recommend a travel route, or share a fresh catch because, for full-timers especially, the campground wherever they stop IS their neighborhood, having the advantage that it changes periodically when the group next door has been getting a little loud.

The magazine version of RVers is a carefully greying couple kicking up their heels in the last festive blow-out of life. Oh, they're out there. And they're having a great time. But there are also many other kinds of people who have brought families or friends, are chasing the surf, or writing books, conducting Internet businesses, or fleeing bills or the law. There are the young wealthy and the old work-campers, the rare hipsters in their art-mobiles, and coaches full of sportsmen towing 16-foot trailers bursting with gear. Every shape, color, and stripe of RVer is out there now, making the road a very interesting place if you're willing to talk. They have left the societies they know, their kids with lousy luck, or their own certain futures, for varying vistas and experiences.

And let's face it, your vehicle really does live and breathe.

Think of it. When you first climb in, all the smells are strange. If it's new, it's got that plastic off-gassing thing that makes you want to break all the windows and ride with your nose out. But very soon, the smells are what tell you you're home. An old motor home like mine is immediately very intimate. There's what's left of the previous owners, an indescribable mix of roasted meat, favorite sweater, old motor oil, and something unidentifi-able. It's not that it's a strong smell, it's that it's an old smell. And imperceptibly, daily, you are adding to it so that when you get in every next time, a little more of your favorite dishes, the hand cream you use, the blanket that a visiting friend left behind, all penetrate you with their smells as well.

When you rely on a vehicle, her familiar sounds tell you things are ok. When you start the engine, it's a member of the family waking from sleep. When you close the door and the stairs retract as they should, your parent's fastened your seat-belt. When you pull out into traffic and the engine rattles but nothing goes wrong, it's the clanking of steam expanding your childhood radiators. It's hard not to anthropomorphize a vehicle, she seems to have moods and aches and pains. She's someone who has protected you, who's weathered difficulty, and who holds you at night when the wind is howling.

33

Who Are These People?

All of which leads me to one of my favorite features of RV camping. Uniquely, you can pull into a campground for the night in a 16-foot Bambi and wake in the morning to find a $1.2 million rig on your right and a pop-up bursting with kids on your left. How often, in other circumstances, would you find all three households the next evening telling stories and gathered loosely around a campfire watching the kids? Well, not often here either. The wealthy tend to stick to their equipment and all three camping groups will start out by trying to give each other plenty of space and respect. RVers aren't different from most of us in that they know about class differences, but sometimes they just can't help themselves and they'll often find ways – perhaps in a contrary effort to beat expectations – to share if they're in pretty good moods.

Neighbors like these continue to be as pleasantly surprised by these encounters as you or I. They just get better at it than most. We all fall into routines and are subject to prejudice, we have similar resentments and fears, but the proximity in the campground can make for some interesting interactions, some real tension, but also some genuine social delight because, as I said before, RVers tend to be a relaxed, philosophical, and fun-loving lot.

Also, there's something about sharing a very small space in a vehicle with a spouse or kid that sorts the wheat from the chaff. If you're able to, you get over yourself very quickly and try to keep out of each other's way. Even the most curmudgeonly seem to develop techniques for making privacy and looking past the dirty laundry to see the sunset. How do I know this? I did have many guests on my trip and, mostly, I found this to be true for us, too.

For those travelers who have been forced into these circumstances by hard times, the strain is obviously greater. But that doesn't stop humanity from occurring:

I wintered near Mendocino, California, in the Caspar Beach Campground, a friendly, undemanding RV park in a cove peopled by surfers, abalone fisherman, and other wayfarers. I was one of a handful of full-timing households. Of course, on the weekends the place usually filled up with short-hop travelers, but during the week there was a small group of us, changing in membership from month to month, but still recognizable as a group.

One evening I came back to the campground after a day of real estate prospecting and discovered a new addition to the community. It was an old Coachman trailer, the contents already well dispersed and strung with Christmas lights. A couple of scraggly kids careened on bikes too small for them and watched me guardedly.

Next to the trailer was parked a thoroughly used Impala, both front doors open and blaring Led Zeppelin's Houses of the Holy. The two long-haired young men standing next to it greeted me with a wave ... because not much else could be heard. I waved back cheerfully and got into my coach quickly to think twice about my next move.

I was tired. It was dark. I had been looking forward to hearing All Things Considered while meditatively preparing dinner. So that's where I began. I turned on the radio … then I turned it up a little higher … and then, because I couldn't hear it over the music outside, I decided something had to be done:

I walked out to the guys still outside and drinking more of many beers and said, "Hi guys, joining our little family?" (They nodded and smiled uncertainly.) "Listen, I love Led Zeppelin but I'm having trouble hearing my radio in there, do you think you could turn that down?" Immediately, they apologized, offered me a beer, and turned the thing right down, for which I waved from my steps and smiled warmly back. And the thing is, I DO love Led Zeppelin.

What's important about this encounter is not actually this day but all the subsequent days. Their little trailer was the home of a young man and woman, apparently unmarried, and her two kids. From the looks of it, that was all they had. She worked in a restaurant and he was floating. In the days that followed I joked with their kids, the dad brought me fresh crabmeat, and I gave them advice and referrals to local businessmen I had met. We were good neighbors.

I am convinced that that first encounter was about recognition, that a family of kids – including the parents – otherwise feeling invisible, found a way to make their presence known and I found a way to know them. In most other circumstances we would never have been neighbors, never have had to reckon with one another in this way. But it was because of our proximity and the shared winter and the strangeness we were feeling together in what was a new place for all of us that we formed a bond. A tenuous, short-lived bond, it's true, but a bond of sorts all the same.

And there was more color in our cloister. Three spaces down, an artist with a big Chicago accent lined his Class C motor home with canvases rumored to have been painted by number. Across from me in a travel trailer was a pale, middle-aged woman of uncertain history and almost certain alcoholism; and on my other side was a lone female physician in a 5th wheel who was in town for 9 months to attend the local woodworking school. Did we spend a lot of time together? Did we become the "best of buds? No, but there are frequent opportunities, many of which I did miss, to get to know the people around you.

34

What You Can Tell About People from Their Rigs

Oh no, I'm not touching that one.

35

How NOT to Have Guests

One of the great pleasures is having guests in the motor home. The more you travel, the better you will get at predicting who's going to present which problems. It's not that you don't present problems to them, it's that it's your house and you get to choose which tangles to get into with whom. But, as I've implied, you just can't tell precisely what's going to come up.

You'll get to know your optimal visit-length quickly. If you're a fusser, I suppose it's pretty short; even if you can stand it, your guests won't be able to stand you. And I suppose it helps to have a good long stretch in the motor home by yourself first to really settle your fussies down about how the thing operates and what you're likely to run into.

Here's how NOT to do it:

If you really want to jeopardize some old friendships, invite the inexperienced RVers who are already control-freaks and bring them on your first voyages. Offer them no assurance that they can rely on your wisdom and experience, just let them loose in the motor home with inadequate instruction and then blame them when they break the equipment and question everything you do. This works wonders if what you're trying to do is weaken old bonds for your flight into the future.

On the other hand, if you want to alienate friends who have a taste for adventure, invite them for a really short stay and then send them home just as they're getting used to the routine. And remember, no matter how long the visit, once you give some people an inkling of how free they can feel on the road, they'll never stop thanking you ... or they'll never forgive you.

You will learn a lot more about your friends in an RV because their nights will be an open book.

Psychoanalysts have understood for years that the night belongs to the shadow side of our psyches, it's the time when the wiggly, wobbly, wonders of our unconscious take over, when what's unsorted in our minds, the parts we can't censor all the time, and the parts that are truly automatic govern everything we do, our breathing, our sleeping, dreaming and waking, even our emissions.

Friends who will tactfully leave the room to vent in one way or another will not do this at night, not because they don't want to, but because they don't know they're doing it. And the same goes for you. Six people trying to control themselves in a motor home, that's 9' x 34' … I'm not sure what the math is that you'd do here, but you do it. And then some people just don't sleep well and will keep others up.

Of course, you might have arguments, food hoarding, hidden addictions, you might discover a guest's propensity for nose-picking in otherwise private moments, and everyone's favorite, the daredevil sex acts everyone hopes no one else can hear. In a motor home there's no other room to go to and when it's raining out, the cost for discretion is just too great.

People are guarded for many reasons. When they're not, it's usually more fun. But for the ones who can't stand getting to know each other better, RVing can be a real challenge.

My coach sleeps one pair of really friendly people; one pair of really short, really friendly people; and one pair who could be anywhere from extremely friendly to moderately friendly but immodest, depending on whether or not you let them use your gigantic bed or whether you take it apart and let them sleep in the twin beds. I was surprised at how little snoring there was. Or how little I heard. My guests were too polite to comment.

There is nothing more fun than having a pile of people in a cool motor home doing something they never expected to be doing, making discoveries right and left, and warming the shared space with love and laughter. On the other hand, there is nothing less fun than feeling like there is absolutely no way to be comfortable due to the fact that people can't sleep or think or bathe because there's no privacy.

Consider packing a tent for when the number you've got turns out to be too many.

36

A Tour of the Motyho after 6 Months in the Care of an Inexperienced and Distracted Coach-Owner

So here were go again. Let's approach the motor home from the curbside. The stairs are making a left turn. On the prized aluminum skin there are fine scratches left by the caresses of branches passing in the night.

Attempt to open the door. The latch jiggles precariously. Recall that since the exploding door debacle on the highway, the latch has never worked well. Having broken again, it is now merely hanging from a wire designed to fix it to the screen-door on the inside. The only working lock is the deadbolt that turns reluctantly.

Step up. The doormat is ripped at one corner and there are smudges all along the baseboard under the sofa. The lampshade on the fixture over the couch leans to the right because the frame was bent when an unbalanced guest fell against it.

The pink barrel chairs are loaded with maps and unfiled papers. There is a fine mildew growing near the vent on the dashboard. The driver's side window is slightly open because the replacement Plexiglas is ill fitted to the frame.

The stereo source-unit in the dash blinks uncomprehendingly. A couple of months ago it got a little too damp to think.

On its side in the kitchen sink, the hand spray lolls uselessly. If you put it back in the holder it will leak water under the sink. There's a faint smell of chicken from the previous night's dinner.

But really, things are pretty much the same. One of the wonderful qualities of these Airstreams is that they just keep holding on. They creak a little, they need some TLC, but they really roll with you.

Look up front: the Beanie Baby waves from the rear-view mirror, reminding you that you are never too far from home.

37

How NOT to Plan Your Route...And Really Get Where You're Going

If you're on an adventure you can't really know your route. And after a 4,000-mile trip that you have slavishly woven through the lowest elevations, you can certainly afford to relax a little ... right?

RV driver, beware. The trucking, transportation, and map-making industries have gone to a lot of trouble to help you plan ahead. Don't insult them in the following manner:

You've gotten over the Appalachians, the Rockies, the Sierras, you've abided by weight and height restrictions, and kept your rig road-ready and clean. You're just waiting for the weather to cool off before you head to the southwest. Why don't you just nip over to the North Coast of California for a week's layover?

Yeah. Tell me about it.

I put more strain on my motor home in the last three hours of our journey than I had on any single day in a 6-month trip. And that's because I forgot to check the elevations on the map.

I have no trouble navigating tight spaces, my first bobble at the carpet-store notwithstanding. I enjoy maneuvering through unfamiliar terrain on narrow lanes that have been cleared for commercial traffic. But when I found myself in the mountains that separate California Route 101 from the coast road, I knew I was unprepared. So I ran hot with an overheat light blinking on and off, barely able to enjoy one of the most beautiful roads in the country.

Although the route is fine for most RVs, my particular motor home towing too much and with a broken rear fuel pump was just not suited to the kind of sustained demand that the ascents and descents put on her that day. I ran the risk of stalling on a short, blind turn with no flares and no passengers to help me ward off traffic.

Ladies and Gentlemen, this is a very bad idea.

But it landed me in a place that changed my life. And if I had known how hard it was for My Particular Coach to get there, I probably wouldn't have gone.

Modest in height though they are, the Mendocino Range is called mountainous for a reason. The best-driven vehicles on those roads are the logging trucks that have plenty of power and are handily and speedily operated by drivers who could probably do it in their sleep. But it's not well designed for a vehicle that's barely pulling an oversized go-cart. I apologize now to the columns of cars I held up for miles at a time when I dared not pull over until I found an ample-sized turnout because I couldn't risk stalling on a hairpin turn.

I don't know why, but most drivers fail to notice the signs that say, "Slow vehicles must allow others to pass." Some kind of obstinacy takes over, as though allowing someone by would be equivalent to succumbing to the schoolyard bully. I've never been reluctant to pull over; it was my vehicle who refused to stop.

So it was touch and go for a while.

But then the road started to level out. When the coastal redwoods leapt up over me and the daylit forest grew so dark that I had to use the headlights, I could see we were past the worst and into stunning new territory. I ignored the obscene gestures of drivers finally freed to pass and felt like an owl gliding silently through a long, high, night corridor.

We followed the river. The trees suddenly started to clear. Then up over a rise, past the Navarro River Bridge, the darkness opened into …. diffuse platinum light and fog. At the crest of the palisade, the inconceivably wide and bright Pacific wrapped itself around the full breadth of my vision. The mist enveloped us. "Oh my God," was all I could say.

Some miles north, in a small town on the banks of the Pacific, was where my trip ended. It was six months long after all. But it stopped where I'd least expected it.

I just couldn't leave.

Something funny happens to us on the Mendocino Coast. There are a lot of theories about it: the white light, the ambient marijuana smoke, a surfeit of negative ions, I don't know.

I parked my motor home in the Caspar Beach campground. I was still there nine months later, assuming ownership of an antique cottage in historic Mendocino village. That's where I met the man who is now my best friend, lover, and husband, Joe Flower.

But the motyho is parked in storage just a couple of miles away. I change the oil periodically, keep the critters at bay.

We gotta be ready. Ya know?

About the Author and About You

So why would you, a person of dignity, with obligations, maybe a mortgage, a young family, or a little retirement nest egg that you're getting close to spending, why would you even *consider* hitting the road, possibly for a pretty long time? Especially if you've never done anything like it before?

Because you are a person of dignity, with obligations, maybe even a mortgage, a young family, or nest egg who may never have done anything like this before! What are

you waiting for? It's never the wrong time to surprise yourself.

OK, you have your reasons. I'm sure they're all very reasonable. You may have been working your butt off trying to make a living. Or trying to find a job. Or you're coming down the home stretch to retirement. Or you've managed to retire and there you are thinking, "Now what?" I'm going to tell you a little of my story and you see if it sheds any light on yours.

Like many 46-year-olds I woke up after 20 years in a profession without having found a lot of what I had been hoping for. I had always assumed that life would somehow deliver the stuff that so many people take for granted. For me they were just a few, oh, small things like finding the love of my life and having children.

Now I know that to you it may feel like some of these things just happen, that you get drawn into relationships or jobs without really resisting them. But as we all come to find out, some things don't just happen for you by accident, they don't happen because they fall on your head, they happen because you allow them to. They happen because you make them happen.

Whatever my obstacles were (that's another book, at least), I was clearly too busy doing what was right in front of me. It has always been easier to do what I know how to do, the other stuff apparently requires some effort and planning.

I guess I've never been much of a planner.

At the time of the attacks on the World Trade Center in New York on September 11, 2001, I was sitting with a patient on Manhattan's Upper West Side, minding his own business. I didn't have any big dreams, I had gotten accustomed to what I was missing in my life. Focusing on my patients helped distract me. I had gradually become the nice (or relatively nice) lady on 93rd Street who lived and would die in her therapist's chair while doing what was expected of her.

And then the planes hit. I realized I actually could end up as a pile of embers never having had any of the experiences I hadn't bothered to make happen. I realized that something had to change, that I had better not wait to be catapulted by a shock wave into a new way of life. I might not survive it.

I finally realized that after years of believing that I had to keep saving or keep working or keep whatevering until I could finally do what I wanted, I recognized I had Enough. I had Enough money, I had Enough energy, I had Enough years left, and I finally had Enough courage to get off my ass and get on my horsey and ride. So I gradually closed my practice, sold my home-office, and set out on a Who Knows What adventure *without even knowing at the time what I was looking for.*

And sure, I got into a few scrapes, spent some afternoons by the side of the road, and made a fool of myself more than a few times. But I did manage to leave a way of life that was beginning to strangle me and, having broken free, I did indeed find a transforming love and a new life that continues to delight and surprise.

And, of course, now I am perfect and never feel sad or confused or fat.

So now you are saying, "Well that's easy enough for you to say, I can't afford to just throw my life up in the air and hit the road!" Well, surprisingly more than you'd expect, RVing is a pretty equal-opportunity kind of adventure. What I mean is that if you're married or single, rich or poor, there's someone out there just like you doing the RV road-trip thing.

For some people, it's an ingeniously cheap but fun way of life. They've got a well used rig, maybe just a little camper on the back of their pick-up or a camper van, and they're out there work-camping (getting jobs along the way). There are couples with young kids in modest-sized motor homes that they bought with the money they would have spent on the last few payments of their foreclosed homes. They're running Internet businesses and homeschooling. There are artists and writers who don't want to spend most of their waking moments numbing their creative minds in boring jobs and instead live on a shoestring in a teardrop trailer so they can do their art (if it doesn't require a lot of room). And there are academics on sabbatical, unemployed workers combing the country for jobs, and retirees who've sold their homes and bought the last domicile they'll own before assisted living near their kids.

For my particular adventure, I bought a very old, cheap, and big motor home, knowing I was saving money on the purchase but that I'd spend it on the breakdowns. For me, the breakdowns and the learning were part of the experience, part of a process that would carry me to situations and people I would never would have encountered otherwise. That's how I engineered some surprises. And it worked!

Your trip will be different. You will take more or fewer risks and make different choices. You may be poor but pretty handy or you may be wealthy with no mechanical skills at all. You may choose to sublet your rented apartment or sell your home thereby saving a lot while you travel. Understand that any way you choose will involve risk. Everybody takes his or her particular risk when he or she leaves what's familiar. Remember who you are and that you bring different strengths and weaknesses to your travel experiment. The road is a place of change and opportunity.

Now that you've finished How NOT to RV you could probably use a little more encouragement from the people in your life to get on the road. If you know someone who might support you (or come with you!) in your quest, you may want to get them a gift of this book, in some form. If they read this book they will either say, "What, are you nuts?" Or, if they have a sense of humor, they will plead, "Can I come?"

You won't be alone. You can come to our site, HowNOTtoRV.com/tellit and share your inevitable goofs. The community of imperfect people is building! When we get enough funny or inspiring stories of RV blunders we'll publish the collection so that your tale will live on to inspire others. Just go to HowNOTtoRV.com/tellit and leave your email address, your name, and your story (which we may edit for flow and humor).

Invite your RVing friends to visit our website to tell their stories too. They don't have to have read the book but of course it helps. Anyone whose tale is included in a new collection will get a free edition of the book and a hat certifying the contributor as an official How-NOT-to Guide.

And if you want to become an Elite How-NOT-to Guide, go to http://HowNOTtoRV.com/elite and learn how. You may have what it takes!

So, dear reader and fellow goof-ball, Happy Trails!

Don't be a stranger!

And don't forget to check the oil.

For More Information

Go to HowNOTtoRV.com.

You know what they say, trust your heart and the rest will follow.

Well, what I say is, trust your heart and fasten your seatbelt!

HOW ^Not TO RV REDUX

RVing for the RVer Who Never Learns

A HOW ^Not TO GUIDE™

"Conquering Fear One Failure at a Time"

Jennifer Flower, Ph.D.

How NOT to RV Redux

RVing for the RVer Who Never Learns

For Readers Conquering Fear

One Failure at a Time

Jennifer Flower, Ph.D

This is a How-NOT-to Guide
For readers conquering fear one failure at a time

This book is not intended as a substitute for good advice. Taking it literally
will get you into a heap of trouble. If you are seriously considering following the instructions in this guide, you should see a psychologist, but probably not Dr. Jennifer Flower.

Table of Contents

A How-NOT-to Guide Rides Again!

So, Dear Reader, you may well have read my first book, <u>How NOT to RV: An RVer's Guide to RVing in the Absurd</u>. It's truly and yet not-so-truly a how-to guide and certainly a way to frame your expectations for what *could* actually happen on your RV road trip … and what to do about it.

But even if you haven't read my first book, you could be considering the titles to that book and this book and be asking yourself whether it's really possible that a driver could never learn, or a trip could be so very absurd.

By now you may be wondering, "But how does a trip really go? I mean, start to finish? Is everything really as silly as this recovering psychologist describes? I mean, surely, even a vaguely sensible person would not suffer so many ridiculous developments in the course of, say, a relatively short transit from one United State to another?

Hmmmmm.

Well, there are a lot of different kinds of people in the world — despite our tendencies to divide them into two kinds — and the blessing is that if you have an open mind, you can learn from most of those kinds of people. You don't have to be an idiot to learn from an idiot, and you don't have to be smart to learn from someone smart.

And you don't even have to decide what learning was until way after the fact. Cogitate on that over your morning coffee.

So, in the interests of entertainment and any residual wisdom that may be gleaned, I've decided to pull back the curtain on how things really went on one particularly memorable trip from Sebastopol, California to Portland, Oregon.

Let's Set the Stage

It's now, what? Well over ten years since the events of the first <u>How-NOT-to-RV</u> book.

Yup. I'm still happily married. My husband is a saint. Most of the time.

We don't live in Mendocino any more.

We spend a lot of our time on a big friggin' 350-ton tugboat!

We are partners in our business. He is a healthcare futurist. No, I had never heard of one either. I've been doing other stuff too. Go to JenniferFlower.net to find out more about that.

Where Joe and I live could change, you never know. But one thing that hasn't changed is the yen for the open road.

So recently I picked up my skirts and jumped back in the Ole Gal again. Yay! Yup, I've still got 'er, a 1986 Airstream motor home, 34.5 feet of glinting aluminum and questionable furnishings. We (everything the Ole Gal and I do together makes We) lit out for the shining city on a major fault line, Portland, Oregon – Yay Boo.

Why Yay Boo? Because if this trip wasn't a study in How-NOT-to, I don't know what is.

Of course, I had to share it with you.

There are a few quite reasonable ways I prepared for my journey to Portland in my vintage Airstream motor home. And I made quite a few mistakes. Let's see which you can identify along the way. You'll have a way to check your answers later.

A Great Excuse for a Trip

So I'm here in my big ole tugboat with my yummy ole hubby and we get the word that our kids are moving to Portland. Boo. But they want us to move up there with them cuz they're gonna have a family. Yay.

So what do we do? We end up buying a floating home slip on the Columbia River.

Are we really moving to Portland? Who knows? Can we now, if we want to? Yes! As soon as I can fit my webbed feet on over these sneakers.

The slip comes with a big RV parking space where we can keep the motyho (a/k/a the Ole Gal). But I have to get her up there. It's a great excuse for a road trip because then I get to go visit the kids in their charming new home that's full of architectural detail. What could go wrong?

First, I recognized that my motor home had been sitting in the storage area for some time. But I wasn't too worried because I had already done some work on her. Extensive work. I had replaced some of the rusting brake lines, the master cylinder, and the rear fuel pump.

That was, oh, a year before.

Actually, I didn't do it, the nice man at the garage did.

He also did a tune-up, changed the oil, and reset the timing to meet California's stringent emission standards for a vehicle of this type and age. After he wiped his hands with the dirty rag that all mechanics have attached to their hands, he stood aside and sent me off in the motyho to the DMV for a smog check.

When the coach stalled right outside the garage, I restarted her, turned around and he reset the timing again.

When I made it up the street and stopped for the nice lady pushing a baby carriage, the motyho stalled again. Back to the garage. He reset the timing again.

When I drove out of the garage, turned the corner, made it through the next intersection, and stopped for the man walking six dogs, she stalled again.

The Ole Gal might not make it on California's terms. At least not as long as there are pedestrians.

I went back to the garage and he reset it again and we just barely squeaked through. Yes, she wouldn't perform as well as she used to, but I didn't have time to dwell on this.

So, I took The Ole Gal down the street to the next stop on the repair list, the Airstream modder guy.

This gentlemanly fellow tidily attired in Dockers and a button-down shirt walked all over the motyho roof, being careful to step only on the riveted seams. He did some poking and sealing and made many approving noises and pronounced her ready for the elements.

Then I parked her in the farmyard spot generously offered by our friends in Sebastopol. She looked right at home among the goats and farming implements. If you squinted hard from a distance.

Taking Your Selves Along

When I realized a year later that I was about to head to Portland, I said to myself as I sat in my living room, "Self, you had a lot of work done last year to bring the motyho up to speed but you really should take a look around her again. In fact, you should take her back to the mechanic right now, just in case."

And then my other Self said. "Naaaah."

And then I did what some might say was a dumb thing. I decided I'd do the once-over myself because, though I am neither a modder nor a mechanic, I have learned a lot, albeit at the arm's length from which many of us learn about vehicles, thinking, "Oh for God's sake, I've got to delegate or my head will blow off."

And besides, I'd had a LOT of work done on her and that had been only a year or so before.

AND this was not my first rodeo. (The self-justification section ends here.)

So I went back up to the farm, picked my way among thistles and blackberry bushes to where my trusty coach was resting, pulled myself up into my rig, lacking the electric steps I had wrapped around a concrete post years before.

I searched inside, checking old leaks, and noticed no new spots on the upholstery, no mold, no carcasses of opportunistic moths craving water, no cloud of tiny gnats that flew up my nose the last time I was inside and that had also nested and died in the crevices of my mattress and encrusted my moisturizer in my bathroom cabinets.

Then I wandered aimlessly through the interior, rediscovering fabrics I had stored there for the next design project, my favorite hand-painted ceramic plates, the quirky mugs, the big bouquet of fake flowers that I put on the doghouse to obscure the dashboard when we're camped, and the propane fire ring.

I threw myself on the bed-the-width-of-the-coach and gazed up through the dirty skylight.

I marveled at how faded The Ole Gal looked and yet how much I still loved her.

I love that coach and I love the dream.

So I went back to the car and packed the following into my rig (Joe would pick up the car later):

- A cache of 85% organic chocolate. Notice this is first on the list.

- My iPad for tunes. Notice this is second on the list. I didn't want to rely on my iPhone for tunes because I didn't want to run down the phone battery.

- The leftover lamb from the meal the night before. I'm on the Paleo diet and we cave-people need flesh to gnaw on rather than be seduced by those nasty, luxurious carbs you'll find waving their arms at every truck stop.

- My thermos of water. Right, Paleo eaters?

- All the goodies I was bringing to our kids in Portland.

- Heave-ho the old standard-issue barrel chairs and replace them with hob-nailed leather club chairs. Generally speaking, this kind of lifting is better done with one other person. But since One Other Person was unavailable, I did this by myself and brought the ibuprofen.

- I slid my suitcase under the bed. I'd unpack that later.

Then I clambered down and added a couple of bottles of fuel treatment in case there was water in the fuel lines, and topped up the oil and checked the tire pressure which, amazingly, was good. I walked the perimeter to make sure nothing was growing into or out of the pipes and vents, and that the hydraulic jacks were appropriately wired up in place so they wouldn't fall down, as they're inclined to, when least expected.

I insinuated myself under the motor home and gazed uncomprehendingly at the chassis. Nothing was intolerably rusty, dripping, or dangling. A good sign.

I got in the driver's seat and started 'er up. It was a little rough. And then she hummed.

Flowers bloomed in my heart.

It took the usual 20 minutes for the carbureted engine to warm up and all the moving parts to get reacquainted with each other, but the choke released, the oil pressure came up to par, the vacuum looked good, the signals worked, and the dead flies in the cup-holder didn't object.

There is nothing like this feeling.

My heart swelled, and my eyes glistened, and when our dear farmer-friend, Bill, host-of-the-RV, and scion of a noble California founding family saw me and asked, "Ready?!"

And I said, "Yup!"

I climbed into the driver's seat, listened for all the right noises, and then nosed onto the country lane and tested the brakes. No problem.

In my rear view mirror I can see Bill wave hopefully, and then the farm disappeared around the corner.

In the side pocket are my necessities – my wallet, my phone, the chocolate, my lip gloss, and my iPad.

Everything now seems so small on this narrow country road. I'm up at bird's-nest level, startling chicks mid-squawk.

At the junction, I pull out into traffic after making way for the Lotus speeding toward me. And then there I am driving on a blue highway, as you do when going on an adventure. Singing.

Yes. I'm singing along with the tunes that I've frenetically plugged into my headset while at the stop sign, and I'm setting my route on GPS, a gift that the geeks have improved greatly since I first got into this RVing thing.

I'm tugging on the Plexiglas driver's side window, a poor substitute for the original glass that broke long ago.

It's not really hot out yet but I want to feel and smell the country breeze and petrochemicals from the farms and vehicles I'll be passing.

And I'm noticing that I'm leaving a couple of hours later than I hoped.

What the hell, no biggy. But I do have a goal and the goal is to get to Ashland, Oregon, before nightfall.

Can we still do it?

Probably.

We (there's that team again, me, the motyho, and, of course, any stowaway rodents and insects) are heading east from Sebastopol in Sonoma County, rolling along verdant country roads where the site of an old quirky Airstream is not that surprising.

This is the seat of the Maker movement, the founders live right down the road. Up ahead there's a camp populated by huge colorful sculptures welded of found objects. They squat on top of buildings, teeter at the edge of mocked up archways, and line the driveway awaiting further work.

I wish I could stop to poke around, but I just love the way this rig feels, floating along on an admittedly compromised suspension.

I learned on my last adventure in the coach that I'd have to say goodbye to the punctured air-bags, so we disconnected the air suspension and replaced the rear leaf springs. I only notice the difference when I go over a ...

BUMP!

Rattle, Clang, Crash!

My carefully arranged objects sidle a little closer to the spots they seem to prefer, and the closet door slams open, obscuring my view through the rear window.

I pull over to prop the door open again. Did I mention that The Not So Nice guy who replaced the suspension also broke my back-up camera so I really do need to see out the back window?

Never mind, back-up cameras are for sissies, I tell myself, as I turn back onto the road that soon smoothes to fresh new black macadam.

I check my mirrors. They're just right. Objects around me move from one mirror to the next. There's only a blind spot of about 30 degrees behind me. Well, isn't this RVing stuff all about moving forward and not dwelling on the past?

I turn onto the interstate and settle in for the long haul north. I zone out for a while because it's starting to get hot. I've resisted turning on the ceiling a/c because it's noisy and a gas hog. I pick out a good podcast about human foibles that will keep me entertained. I take stock.

Is it time for lunch yet?

Nope.

Is it time for snacks yet?

Nope.

Just then, my thermos falls off the doghouse and comes to rest under the gas pedal.

I lean over, grunt, and barely manage to free it as I slow for some traffic.

As I straighten up, I glance left to see a van full of kids cheering and giving me the thumbs-up. And a soccer mom smiling with relief to see that my coach has a driver.

I, of course, grin, and, as I wave back, toss water out of my thermos and all over my left shoulder.

On the Road Again, Bumpity Bump

Why do people wave at old Airstreams? I don't really know.

The funny thing about my coach is that from behind she looks almost dainty, with her tidy rounded rear end, little round tail-lights, and the skirt I added that demurely protects her nether parts and the windshield of my Toad (the vehicle you tow).

No Toad on this trip!

But then you start to pass me and then the coach seems impossibly longer than you would expect, something about the proportions and the unembellished skin, she just keeps going and going and going, which leaves most people, even me, when I'm walking past her, filled with awe and delight. She's like a foot-long hotdog with those extra bites that you always wish you had with a regular one.

Then, oddly, when you get to the front she just looks silly. The cab is a complete anticlimax. I suspect the folks who designed these motor homes were the same ones who designed the trailers and you know what the front of a trailer looks like, right?

Not much.

What probably happened when they got to the design for the motyho front was Carl said, "OK, Bob, where's the sketch for the cab?" and Bob said, "I thought you had it!"

And they slapped one together.

I guess there's something game and cool and silly and lovely about Airstreams. I'm just happy we make other people happy.

No matter, it's a lovely warming day.

I'm too lazy to stop for lunch but I'm definitely getting hungry now. My stomach is starting to drown out my tunes.

Hey wait! I almost forgot! Emergency chocolate!

I root around in the side pocket next to my iPad where I thoughtfully stored my chocolate …

and come up with a gooey brown mess.

I guess even M&Ms would have had a hard time under these conditions.

Not only has the cab been hot, but the iPad has been throwing off heat which has concentrated in this enclosed space on the one thing I most needed to keep cool because: It's EMERGENCY chocolate. It's the chocolate you fall back on when all else fails or you're too lazy to get your doughy ass off the driver's seat and get some lunch.

But now it seems that it's my iPad that has fallen back on the chocolate.

Or, really, into it.

I withdraw the tablet from the pocket to reveal a puddle of the confection that has nicely molded itself into the device's speakers and jack.

Oh Fate! Oh dismal world! Oh sole mio (cue orchestra)!

I quickly turn off the tunes because I don't want to cause a short in the iPad while using the electricity.

So now I'm crabby. I pull over for lunch, the pleasure of which is overshadowed by the Tragic Loss of Chocolate and Tunes.

Back in the coach, I connect my headphones to my iPhone and discover that the dashboard 12-volt chargers are not working. Not one of them. And when I stop and pull the fuse, it doesn't look burnt. But I also notice I have no more fuses.

So I'm back in the saddle and steaming up Route 5. We are heading into more mountainous territory now and soon we're careening gaily around the S-curves, snaking our way into the Siskiyou mountains.

On the bridge crossing Shasta Lake we are met with an appalling sight. There's so little water in the lake that the pontoon boats are clustered like frightened horses in a too-small corral.

This might be a good time to buy a cheap pontoon boat.

The other noticeable change is the air is getting a mite smoky. I check the weather ahead and it's pretty clear. Except for the fires.

And where are the fires, you may ask?

Well, they're right around the aptly named Ashland, my camping destination.

I resolve to make better time. If I get there early enough and the conditions are really bad, I can still change my plan. But I'm reluctant to change my plan because I've already paid for the campsite – I think, I can't remember. But there's no cell phone service here for calling ahead to check on the situation.

I'd rather not do my overnight stop before Ashland because the prevailing winds are carrying the smoke in this direction. And besides, I want to make a lot more headway today so that I'll have more freedom of movement in Portland tomorrow.

So we keep pushing on and on, up and up, the coach sailing easily on the smooth surface, the occasional passing car of vacationers waving and smiling.

But I'm getting hungrier and hungrier again.

I look at the map. There's a nice little town up ahead, Dunsmuir. Maybe I can gas up and get some cell phone service and eat my precious lamb.

That's exactly what I find, a nice place under the trees where I can pull over, a gas station that will still be open after I finish my dinner, and a teeny weeny bit of cell phone service.

We gracefully lurch onto the shoulder, I put 'er in Park, engage the emergency brake, jump out of the driver's seat, and yank open the fridge …

To discover a warm, smelly package of oozing leftovers remonstrating me silently.

Why, oh why, didn't I turn on the fridge?

Oh wait. But I DID turn on the fridge. I flipped the switch. The light came on. But apparently, it was just the light. No cooling has been taking place.

Very bad news indeed.

OK, so I make the best of what I've got, and I call the campground. They say, of course, that conditions aren't too bad.

For what? Complete asphyxiation?

I choose to believe them. I choose to, because I'm ready to leave the scene of this last debacle for greener, if smokier pastures ahead.

I get in the driver's seat, put on my pointless seatbelt, turn the key and …

Nuttin.

Oh, the engine almost turns over, but not quite.

I have vapor lock.

I have vapor lock because, as I now realize, somewhere between home and here the rear fuel pump stopped working. Yes, the new fuel pump has died.

Vapor lock, as you may recall, is what happens when your rear fuel pump is offline and you happen to stop long enough for the heat to accumulate in the fuel lines, vaporizing the fuel because there's no longer the cooling effect of high-speed air.

I could possibly camp here. But I know what's going to happen. At three in the morning someone will rap on my door with a big stick. I will shake myself from a troubled sleep, sure that it's mountain marauders. It will turn out to be the police, asking if everything's OK which it may or may not be, and then I won't be able to get back to sleep.

I just want to get to Ashland. Is that too much to ask? I need more chocolate!

But first the fuel has to turn back from vapor into fluid. And I don't know how long I'm going to have to wait.

And it's getting darker.

I call my husband for solace. He comforts me in that distant voice he gets when he's thinking, "There she goes again!" while he's making a post on social media.

Don't get me wrong, he's quite sympathetic. But what can he do?

All there is to do is wait.

But today is my lucky day! Sort of. It only takes 45 minutes!

I've got the engine running again, I've got a belly full of tepid lamb, and I'm off.

I pull back into traffic.

Now it's full-on evening. The sun setting through the growing haze makes for a ghostly landscape, drained of color. There are bands of smoke like fog in the air except this fog is many shades of ecru and brown. The smell is unmistakable. I stop trying to tell myself it's fog.

Definitely not the best air for breathing.

This stiffens my resolve. I'm going to get to Ashland, and beyond if I have to.

I want to breathe the sweet air of freedom!

Sorry, sometimes I get carried away with travel rhetoric.

The way is going to be easy through the remaining Siskiyou mountains. I remember this route. Or I think I remember, because it looks familiar.

Then we start up a longer, straighter section of Route 5, that snakes up much steeper, longer grades.

I don't remember this part.

There are some landmarks that look vaguely familiar, but the increasingly long rising grades seem as though they have been transplanted from some other part of the country. Where I haven't been.

Turns out, everything looks different in a 34-foot motor home from the way it looks in, say, the 1999 BMW M3 that Joe and I drove the last time we took this route.

So every time I start up another rise, I have to concentrate on loosening my grip on the wheel. Pushing is not going to help.

Every step of the way another episode of vapor lock is still possible.

The landscape gets smokier, the visibility drops, and fewer cars are on the road. And definitely fewer RVs. It's just me and the big rigs hauling at 20 mph up the long grades.

To make matters worse, there is construction along much of the roadway that now narrows to one lane and leaves no shoulder where a broken down motor home could demurely wait for sunrise or a tow.

I picture myself stopping dead in the middle of traffic, obstructing half the interstate commerce in this part of the world.

I guess that's one way to attract assistance.

The Ole Gal strains, but she does not die. I guess the ambient temperature is so low that the gas is staying liquid and the engine temp stays low, despite the heavy demand.

And it is beautiful. Unlike any other landscape I've seen. The smoke gives the now-rising moon a dulled, eerie quality. Tendrils of fresher, white smoke stream across it, while sootier haze pools is low-lying areas, underlit by homes below.

It's quiet, too. Except for the occasional growl of an 18-wheeler, I feel like I am sailing through a foamy dream, in which distances are jumbled up, complicated by irregular stripes of light and shadow.

Now there is so little traffic that I have to strain to see the road because our 28-year-old headlights are tired and ready for a permanent nap.

My phone is close to dead, I have to save it. No more power for my music. We bring in a local radio station and get only promises of redemption, threats of eternal damnation, or rasping balladeers whom I cannot hear well enough to sing along with, even if I recognized their songs.

I call the campground in Ashland. The vaguely sympathetic lady tells me that I can come in as late as I need to, that they'll leave my info packet on the board outside the office. Routine for late campers.

She can't tell me how long it will take to get there.

All that is left is surrender. It's 10 pm. Then 10:30 p.m. The grade has lessened and I settle philosophically into the rhythm of the gentler mountain curves.

At around 11:15 I come to the exit, and turn onto a peaceful, undulating country lane, definitely in the opposite direction of the town of Ashland I hoped to walk to in the morning for breakfast.

I find the campground easily. It's charming and rustic. There is a tidy white office with a night light on the porch. To get to it, I cross a little arched wooden bridge over a pond with sleeping fish. I pick up my packet and perch on the bench to read it. My site is just around the corner.

Things are starting to look up.

So I get back in my rig and start down the path indicated by the map. And then I get to the end.

So I start back around the loop.

I cannot for the life of me see my site.

So I start back around, more slowly this time, and notice only a very dark hole on the left which, surely, is not my site.

And I get to the end and have to circle back around. With an engine running rough at 11:30 at night when everyone else is trying to sleep.

So I start back around and this time I stop in front of the black hole and walk in with my flashlight.

At the back of the site is a teeny tiny little site number and a big, dark green picnic table.

I cleverly put the flashlight facing outward on the picnic table, get back in my coach and check the mirror. I can see the flashlight.

I put her in reverse, confident of my path and proud of my resourcefulness ...

Except for the really loud scraping noise as I bump and push the picnic table deeper into the site.

I manage to notice before the hard stop that is a tree, and I immediately pull forward and adjust.

I guess I was too tired to remember to put the light on the attached inner picnic *bench* so I'd see the point closest to my rig.

No one laughs. There's that.

It is so dark and I am so tired that all I hook up is the electricity so I can plug in my phone. Marvel of marvels, the fridge starts right up.

I shuffle into the campground bathroom, do the minimum, and shuffle back out. I open the lid in the bedroom to let in just a little of the contaminated air, and then throw myself on the unmade bed-the-width-of the-motor-home, among garbage bags of clothes and the propane fire ring.

And sleep like a waterlogged tree stump.

The Light of Day Reveals Only So Much

The next morning is smoky, it's true, but we campers are all still breathing and mostly unmarked by flying embers. At the local breakfast place I eat a lot of everything.

Ashland is a charming town. No joke. It's worth stopping there if you love comfy restaurants with good, often organic food; a lovely snaking path through a carefully tended park where you can walk off your meal and take selfies with ducks; and frequent performances of Shakespeare plays or, if you're lucky, the full-on Shakespeare festival that attracts visitors from far and near.

At least I've heard that this is true because I never made it into Ashland that day because of all the other screw-ups.

So right after breakfast we're back on the road again, easy as pie!

It is just a little farther to the main stretch of highway heading into Portland. The mountains have settled down somewhat, and Grants Pass, which sounded intimidating, is a non-event. The hours breeze by, no problem.

The smoke has cleared, we emerge from the mountains, and then we enter the straight stretch approaching the city where of course everyone's speed picks up because suddenly everything is so damned important.

I start to think about the campground near downtown Portland and the hazard of approaching it during rush hour on a hot day.

In a rig that gets vapor lock. When stuck in traffic.

That is definitely something to be avoided if at all possible.

I am strategizing about this, humming a little tune, when …

THTHTHTHTHTH-UMP! WAP-WAP-WAP-WAP-WAP-WAP!

The coach starts pulling to left!

As I yank myself back into my lane, I see in my side mirror that my driver's-side awning has unrolled into 70 mile-per-hour traffic, threatening to put a part in the hair of the big-rig driver who was at that moment attempting to pass me.

I gradually pull to the shoulder, praying there is enough of one.

And stop.

The vehicles behind me immediately start to merge into the fast lane when they can. But some can't do it fast enough.

We all manage to avoid causing a northbound pile-up.

I turn on the flashers and jump out to sneak around the nose of my rig, where I peek first at the startled faces of oncoming drivers and then at the damage.

The awning is extended as though it were time for tea.

It's too high for me to reach.

I grab a footstool from inside and flatten myself in the best Buster Keaton fashion against the driver's side of the coach, standing precariously on the footstool, my skirt billowing out into traffic.

For moments like these there should always be a dramatic orchestral upwelling, don't you think? Or at least a laugh track?

But there is nothing but the roar of passing vehicles, the occasional honk, and lots of flapping noise.

And nothing to secure to anything else. There is no gap to run a bungee cord through to keep the awning from unfurling and I don't have a long enough rope to tie onto the awning brackets and then toss over the coach to secure it to the other side.

I examine the supports and notice that a key piece of the strut on the forward end is not in place. It's not even in evidence. Where is it? I have no clue. There's some of the strut left in the front, but not enough structure to wrap with tape.

I roll the spring-loaded awning back up as tightly as I can and secure the struts on the aft end with a short bungee cord. But it's a long awning and the front is still vulnerable to getting sucked open by the vacuum from passing trucks.

After a hasty search inside for the missing part with no good results, I decide I'd better just get back on the road. It's dangerous to be in so large a vehicle on so narrow a shoulder. The highway patrol will move me along as soon as they can. Without a compelling reason to be there, like total breakdown, I will not be the object of their sympathy.

Once back on the road, everything seems fine. The awning doesn't shake. I'm just starting to regain my confidence when another big rig passes me at 80 miles an hour.

THWAP! WUP-WUP-WUP!

The awning unrolls again, this time crooked, extended just from the forward end, like a huge broken party horn that doesn't honk.

The awning is my magnificent banner for the How-NOT-to Guide that I am.

Scares the living daylights out of me. But there is no exit yet. We've got to tough it out.

At the next opportunity to stop, I jump out, brazenly stick my butt back out into traffic, reroll the awning and get back in the coach, doing 3 Hail Marys under my breath, which probably wouldn't work because I'm not even Catholic.

When the front of the awning unapologetically unrolls again about 5 miles down the road, another moment of surrender comes …

To a local Airstream service department which, thankfully, turns out to be 15 minutes away on a side road! And here's the exit now!

Is there a She-being, or what?

I pull in at the last minute before the service department closes, call our kids who pick me up in the Mini (yes, the same bright blue Mini I towed into <u>How-NOT-to-RV</u> fame 13 years earlier), and am deposited within a half hour in their back yard with a cold drink.

We believe in driving our vehicles into the ground.

Clearly.

So that's how I ended up popping Claritin and living for a long weekend with my step-son and his wife and their two cats. I had a great time. I love them all but I'm allergic to the cats' dander. Probably not to the kids' dander, though.

The next day the repairs begin and continue for months on and off, long after I had flown home:

- Faulty spring on the awning? Fixed.

- Rusty propane tank? Replaced with a nifty removable tank for easier filling.

- Cabinets that kept jumping between me and my view through the back window? Fixed

And other assorted items, per usual.

After they had finished with what they could do, the nice Airstream people then got my coach to a mechanic who informed me that an electrical problem was causing the rear fuel pump to fail. On old rigs, the electrical grounds are often corroded. They will cause mayhem with any and all your electrical circuits. Don't replace a lot of expensive other stuff unless or until you've checked, or had them check, the electrical grounds.

Having solved the electrical problem, the mechanic could then fix the fuel pump problem, and therefore the vapor lock problem! Yay! No more swapping in new fuel pumps every year or so!

He also fixed a few other things, and ordered a new wiper assembly so I could drive in the rain without using the Braille method.

Then a very nice person parked my rusting motyho in our RV space in Portland, one of the dampest but most charming major cities on the West Coast.

STOP! Shall We Review? And Actually Learn Something?

OK, so I'm not perfect. At all.

Maybe it's never a good idea to leave in a hurry, but sometimes we humans just do. Sometimes it's because we have to Get Out or Get There for "real" reasons like, say, fire and deadlines.

But other times it's just the urgency we feel for Getting Out There. No matter how hard some of us try, we can't be Mr. or Ms. Sensible about getting back on the road. Especially when we have vintage rigs that can slow the preparation process down unexpectedly.

After a while, we and our wallets just lose the enthusiasm for being systematic and we say to ourselves, we say, "Screw perfection. There are some things I can't control, and some things I can't afford to make sure I prevent. I just have to get my ass on the road."

So we do. We do it knowing that we will run into Problems and that we will have to solve them on the way.

It's kind of like Life.

Besides, the unpredictable is one of the reasons many RVers go RVing, remember?

Here's the thing. If you're going to leave in a hurry, AT LEAST USE A CHECKLIST! Go online and do a search for RV checklist, or better yet, "travel trailer checklist" or "motor home checklist" or whatever new or ancient model you may have. Different vehicles warrant different checklists and rig models change over the years so any checklist I will give you will be outdated quickly.

I had forgotten my checklist. I even forgot that I had a checklist.

It had been two years since I'd driven anywhere more than a half hour in the motyho. I'd gotten out of the habit of using a checklist.

Bad Idea.

But in my case? I got a lot right without one. And nothing went wrong for a while except the kinds of things you miss when you're in a bit of a hurry and the new things that never happened before.

Here are some lessons I learned about how to prepare for this trip:

When you plan to put your precious piece of carefully roasted meat in the fridge, make sure the fridge is cold first. This is not that easy to confirm, so if you care, you have to plan ahead to know for sure.

RV fridges cool by a different method from your fridge at home and they don't make the cold noise, but like any fridge, they take a while to get to the point where you can put food in them. And by the way, don't put the food in them and then turn on the fridge! It takes much longer for them to reach the target temp that way.

If you want to make sure your fridge is working, come back five hours after you've plugged it in, or started it up on propane. Feel it. Better yet, use a thermometer that will feel it when you can't. To get the fridge cold enough for food, you'll probably have to run it on propane overnight or on shore power that you have thoughtfully installed on the side of your house where your rig may be parked.

Who wants a great piece of dinner sitting in a tepid fridge for 7 hours while it thinks about cooling off? I didn't, but that's what I got because, the fridge? She no cold.

If you're in a hurry and don't have time to turn the fridge on beforehand, carry the food in a cooler packed with ice and keep the key items in there while the fridge is getting ready to receive them. But still, at least test it.

OK, so where was I?

Back to the checklist. Why is a checklist important? Because without it you don't:

- jam a big storage box in front of the closet door that doesn't stay closed and that swings open at the first turn to block your view through the rear window.

- close the loose ceiling fan lid that rattles and threatens to fly off into traffic.

- test the appliances that have no particular incentive to keep working after decades

- start the fridge the night before and test it in the morning before you put food in it

- write down the particulars of your camping destination, including the actual name of the place, the phone number, and the confirmation number for your payment

Check, or have an RV mechanic (not the guy at the local garage) thoroughly check your critical domestic RV systems before you leave. This usually means you'll have to go to two service centers for all the work you need, the ones who work on the chassis (and engine and drive train), like your local truck or RV garage, and the ones who work on the domestic side of the RVs.

Remember, a year or two is a long time in the life of a 30-year-old vehicle. A lot goes wrong faster and faster, just like with your body, including your brain!

Don't be a cheapskate! Or be someone who knows what you're doing.

If you have a coach vulnerable to vapor lock, make sure they check the rear fuel pump because that's mostly what's between you and a sour ride.

Basically check anything that's given you trouble and anything you suspect might give you trouble this time. And No. You can't possibly know everything.

That means that by now, your checklist will look substantially different from everyone else's checklist, due to the quirks of your particular vehicle. And if you're at least as old as your rig, possibly because you've been together a long time, you must write down the items you used to remember but now you tend to forgot about, like the awning strut you noticed a break in two years ago and thoughtfully stored under your rear bed which is completely inaccessible to a road-weary driver by the side of the road. And besides, I forgot to have it replaced.

And if you have an old rig, you must bring …

Duct tape!

It's the only solution to some of your mid-trip problems. If I'd had some duct tape, I could have taped the awning up at the poles. The way my husband did later.

Oh wait. I did have Duct Tape. I just didn't think of it.

Rule # 946? Think of it!

Beyond the Checklist

It's up to you how much you take on. If you're not a mechanic yourself, you can identify a lot of problems on your own, using your trusty checklist, but you'll still have to get the mechanics to fix them. If you resolutely refuse to learn how to do them yourself.

There are a lot of things you can do if you are willing to learn. Well, OK, that includes everything, but let's be reasonable. You're not going to learn everything.

OK. Well, some of you are going to learn everything, maybe just to prove me wrong, but most of you will put the priority on the experience of RVing and not on being under the RV on a soggy piece of cardboard.

Some of the easy things you can learn to do are testing appliances and electrical sockets and continuity (using a tester, not your finger), and replacing fuses, and cleaning wasps nests out of the water heater cabinet, and winterizing or dewinterizing your rig which usually means running a lot of water through a lot of things for a long time.

But if you are going to end up asking the mechanic to fix stuff anyway, you could spring for the extra hour or so of labor and have them test a lot of those things themselves because their checklist might be different from yours in some important ways.

As I said, you really should have not one but two mechanics, one for the chassis, one for the motor home. Each will go through their safety and convenience checks. I say safety and convenience because there are some things that the RV mechanic will take the time to check that you may forget. Like whether the fridge is actually working and not just whether the light on the fridge is working.

The chassis mechanic might have had a better chance at catching the electrical problem with your rear fuel pump – if you were me and had this problem – but in actual fact, I took my rig to many chassis mechanics over the course of several years, and they just enjoyed replacing the fuel pumps and never caught the electrical problem. Until the guy in Portland did.

Let's Get Real

There are some things that a checklist can't help you with much. Among them are:

- your changing brain, and

- your changing perspectives.

Let's start with your changing brain.

You'll find as you get older that you may still approach some things as a kid. But you may also be a somewhat different RVer at 40 than you were at 30, or at 70 than you were at 50. It takes a mature person to notice that this is a significant difference, but then sometimes people aren't so mature about some things.

Your memory may have changed. I suspect this contributed to some of my errors. I was remembering the problems I had when I first had the motyho and was forgetting some of the more recent ones that only happened once. Older, more rehearsed memories stick around longer, and then of course there are some things you'd prefer to forget.

Memory changes can be quite insidious. When you've done something often, you remember it based on some vague average of your experiences, rather than the few minor irregularities over time.

For example, I've parked at Costco so often that I have a vague average memory of where I parked. I forget where I most recently parked, so now I always park in the row that lines up with the big Costco sign on the side of the building. That means there's only one lane of parking spaces that I have to examine carefully for my car.

Let's consider changes in perspective now.

If you drive somewhere in a small powerful car, you are going to remember it the way that trip went.

But everything looks different in a big rig from the way it looked in the sport coupe you drove the last time you took that route.

The thing is that when you drive a motor home that has limited power due to some mechanical problem that you clearly have not yet solved, the elevations present themselves to you like the build-up of an orchestra in the scary moments of the movie …

Except you don't know how long this movie is going to be.

You cannot tell yourself that no matter how bad this movie is, it's only going to last for another hour because you've never seen this one before.

The movie you saw in your smaller, more powerful vehicle was a jaunty jolly bro trip in which ups and downs were just part of the fun.

Will a checklist help you remember that your drive will be different this time in a different vehicle? Maybe. But come on, folks, let's face it, are most of us going to keep such a thorough checklist? Naaah. Some of us are always going to take our chances.

Why Take Chances?

We're going to take our chances because for some of us, the romance of starting off down the road is partly about serendipity and risk, it's about testing our resourcefulness or just not worrying so much, it's about seeing what we can get away with.

It's about being free.

And being really careful for people like that, is not being free.

I guess the best plan is to have an obsessive-compulsive family member who does all this stuff for you and then doesn't come with you to spoil the adventure.

I trust you. I know you can work it out. I know you can be as goofy as I am, and still have a reasonably safe trip and lots of fun.

What it comes down to, though? We, each of us, human and RV, have a different personality.

The trick to RVing is this: You've got to have your kind of trip, not the safest, or the most exciting, or the most romantic. The idea is to have the trip that you in your you-est you most want to have.

When you look back on your life, you don't want to say, "I did it Ralph's way!"

You want to say, "I did it my way!"

For some people Just Going is the point. For some people being The Expert is the point. For some people being Self Sufficient is the point.

And there are many points of overlap.

What I say is that knowing ThySelf – and for some of us, Thy Selves – is the shortest route to happy RVing. Don't try to be someone you don't enjoy being.

Check?

Get on it!

And don't forget to check the oil!

But There is More to Our Story

Dare I say that a little time has passed since that Portland How-NOT-to trip?

And yes, that we've had quite a few other adventures besides? Both in and out of RVs?

I just can't fit everything I have to tell you in this book.

So stay tuned for the next How-NOT-to-Guide!

I'm pecking away on the little keyboard right now!

I just have to hit

RETURN!!

Be a How-NOT-to Guide

Most trips are not as uh, checkered, as mine was to Portland. You'll certainly have different experiences. Maybe soon. Maybe already. Maybe worse! Come on down to HowNOTtoRv.com/tellit and share your RV travel goofs. Many have before you and I doubt it will hurt and it will probably be fun.

If you're really feeling expansive, and you think you have a How-NOT-to Guide in you, send us five pages of your story about how NOT to do, well, anything, like plant a garden, learn to rollerblade, go sport-fishing, organize a family reunion ... the possibilities are endless.

You don't have to write it in my style or with my structure, but it has to be amusing and useful and show the mistakes you made in your heroic efforts to just learn something new.

Go to HowNOTtoRV.com/elite for instructions on how to submit 5 pages of your story.

If you can tell us about your goofs and victories in enough detail and self-effacing good humor, there's a good chance we'll like it, and contact you to discuss it. Who knows? It could mean your first big break into the Self-Hindrance Literature! If it's a good fit, we'll make you an offer for your story. If we sign you up, we'll also send you a free How-NOT-to-Guides hat when your story is published. If we get enough Guide writers together, well, can you imagine?

Join a proud phalanx of authors boldly striding into the error-strewn future. And if that doesn't appeal to you, use a pen name if you prefer, and write in the shadows wearing your Zorro mask. Sometimes it takes a while to recognize one's true strengths in fallibility. But don't let that story die with you.

See you in the funny pages!

www.ingramcontent.com/pod-product-compliance
Lightning Source LLC
Chambersburg PA
CBHW031544040426
42452CB00006B/177